Dinners in a Dash

SENSATIONAL THREE-COURSE DINNER PARTIES IN UNDER 2 HOURS

Tessa Harvard Taylor

GRUB STREET • LONDON

Dedicated to Nick, Jack and Katie

Acknowledgements

I would like to thank everyone who has contributed to this book but there are a few people in particular to whom I am extremely grateful. First, my Mother, who allowed me to experiment in her kitchen from the age of five when I created my first rock cake recipe. Jack and Katie who have had to spend so much time being patient while "Mummy invents another recipe". To Rebecca Michael, Billie Harris and Barbara Rayner for being a great source of inspiration. To Clare Walker, Michele Breene, Lynville Barratt, Ali Hammond and the late Pam Calton who have assisted me with my cookery demonstrations.

All the people who have helped with recipe testing and proof-reading, especially Susan Hall, Fiona Boardman, Ann Alvis, Tricia Owen, Penny Egan, Jennie Pope, Grasshopper Thompson, Nigel Barratt, Elizabeth Naylor, Moira McNally, Carolyn Russell, Carey Botting and Jillian Aziz.

Anne Dolamore, my patient publisher, for all her help, guidance and understanding of my sense of humour.

Karen Wise at Oddbins who has recommended all the wines for the book.

Gordon "Reg" Parris and his team at Waitrose, Sunningdale who have been so helpful in putting up with my strange requests and locating weird products for me.

The Centre for Living, White Lodge for all their help.

And last, but most importantly, my husband Nick, for all his encouragement and support while eating his way through every recipe in this book, sometimes sampling variations of the same recipe three or four nights in a row!

Published by Grub Street
The Basement, 10 Chivalry Road
London SW11 1HT

Copyright this edition © Grub Street 1998

Reprinted 1998, 2002

First published in hardback by Grub Street 1996

Text copyright © Tessa Hardvard Taylor 1996

Cover photograph: Tim Imrie
Cover design. Adam Denchfield Design
Author's photograph: Jo Mieszkowski

The moral right of the author has been asserted.

British Library Cataloguing in Publication Data

Taylor, Tessa Harvard

Dinner in a dash: how to cheat with flair and confidence
1. Cookery 2. Quick and easy cookery

I. Title
641.5'5

ISBN 1 898 1

Printed and bound in S   .L., D

Contents

INTRODUCTION

Would you like to enjoy entertaining, cook with confidence, use convenience foods without guilt? Yes it's now possible…For those of you who feel obliged to go further than piling a few M & S ready-meals into the oven (apart from the fact that everyone will recognise them) but just haven't got the time or inclination to cook everything from scratch, then this is the book for you. It is designed to show you how to prepare and cook exquisite dinner parties with the minimum amount of time and effort. The recipes teach you a method of mixing convenience foods with fresh natural ingredients. They show you how to create fabulous dinner parties in a fraction of the time your friends would have imagined and convince them that they are completely home-made.

On the other hand, if you are a real gourmet who likes to make puff pastry from scratch, doesn't approve of food processors, only uses wire whisks with copper bowls to whip egg whites, and will spend 24 hours making and reducing the fish stock, then this book is not for you.

I have no formal cooking qualifications, but have talked my way into doing Directors' Lunches and worked as a freelance cook. I cooked in French and Swiss ski resorts for two seasons working as a "Chalet Girl" and spent a summer working in Greece. It is from these experiences that I became skilled at short-cut cooking. My main aim was to spend the maximum time skiing, or on the beach in Greece, and the minimum time cooking but at the same time producing elegant three course dinner parties for my guests. I am now married with six-year-old twins and still enjoy entertaining, which means that I have a vast amount of experience of cooking in a "dash".

Dinners in a Dash started in the form of cookery demonstrations. A complete three-course dinner party for 8 to 10 people is prepared and cooked by me within a maximum of 2 hours. My guests then sit down to enjoy the meal, amidst lively chatter of when they are going to repeat the gourmet experience. A whole new world has opened up and they are inspired by a new concept and the ease with which they will be able to entertain in the future. Due to the popularity of the demonstrations, which I am continuing to run, I have decided to compile a book of my recipes.

I was inspired to create *Dinners in a Dash* for two reasons. One of them was a series of awful dinner parties given by a good friend of mine (I hope the person concerned doesn't realise that I am t'king about her – otherwise it could be the end of a good friendship!). The food was pretty mediocre and, even worse, we didn't see much of our hostess. She spent most of the eveni

in the kitchen and when she did appear, she was extremely harassed.

The second reason was after a conversation with mothers at a local toddler group. 90% of them admitted that they had stopped entertaining since having children because they just did not have the time any more. If only someone could show them some short cuts, they would all actually enjoy giving dinner parties – and that is exactly what I've done.

Gone are the days of serving a choice of four different desserts and then finding you are eating the left-overs for the next week. All my menus include just one dessert and a fresh fruit platter – why waste so much time making the other three when no one eats them? You will also find that most main courses are served with potatoes, rice, etc. and just one other vegetable. Why make extra work for yourself?

I'm sure you will enjoy cooking and eating these recipes and find the book fun. I hope it will provide the impetus to throw away those excuses of why you can't hold a dinner party and enter the exciting and entertaining world of *Dinners in a Dash*.

For more details of cookery demonstrations write to: *Dinners in a Dash*, Kenwolde Manor, Callow Hill, Virginia Water, Surrey GU25 4LF.

10% of all royalties will be donated to The Centre for Living, White Lodge Centre, Holloway Hill, Chertsey, Surrey – a day centre for people with disabilities.

IMPORTANT INFORMATION

All the recipes in the book are set out in groups of complete dinner party menus for eight people. This saves you the laborious task of pouring over recipes working out which starter goes with which main course, vegetables, etc. However, feel free to experiment and 'mix 'n match' menus to suit your mood. The menus are grouped into seasons, using seasonal produce, but in most cases there is no reason why you can't swap them around and cook a spring menu in winter for example. Some of the menus have certain themes, e.g. "A Touch of the Orient", "Italy in an Instant", "Mexico Made Easy". Even though these menus include some typical dishes and ingredients, they are not necessarily genuinely authentic. Authenticity often takes time and these recipes are designed to save time. Many factors have been taken into account when planning menus. For example, colour, oven space, time, "cheatability", calorific value. On the subject of calories, I have mentioned where it is possible to use "low fat" alternatives but in some cases, it just tastes so much better to use the "full fat" version. If you are using these recipes for everyday cooking, then it may be a good idea to use as many low fat substitutes as possible, but for special occasions when entertaining guests, it shouldn't matter if you have a few extra calories.

Most of the recipes are for eight people but they can easily be doubled, halved or, even better, if you are cooking for only four, you can follow the recipes for eight and, where appropriate, freeze half.

AHEAD OF TIME

Most of the recipes can be prepared in advance or frozen. It will indicate in the recipe at which stage this can be done. The following symbols apply where recipes can be prepared in advance:

❋ May be frozen
◖ May be made the day before
☼ May be made earlier in the day

All menus can be prepared in under two hours except where you see a symbol ☆ which indicates that something in the menu needs marinating, cooking, or freezing for over 2 hours.

All the menus can be prepared in under two hours and some take far less time – see "Half an Hour to spare" page 46. If you can be relaxed, you and your guests will enjoy the evening much more and your food will taste even better.

WINE

Wines are recommended with each menu to save you even having to think about what to drink. Most of the wines are priced between £4-£6 a bottle but a few special ones are slightly more expensive. I have suggested a style of wine with each menu, such as a nutty Italian white and then a particular wine, such as Grechetto del Umbria 'Il Vignola' but you can also make your own choice.

SHOPPING

This can be a real chore but you should be able to find everything under one roof if you shop at a large supermarket. If it means going miles out of your way to buy the suggested brands, then don't bother. They are only recommendations and there will probably be other good brands more easily available that you can use.

CONVERSIONS – from metric to imperial are not strictly accurate but are rounded up or down to make the recipes easier to follow. Metric and imperial quantities may be mixed.

EGGS – recipes have been tested using size 2 and 3 eggs. Other sizes will also be fine. No raw eggs have been used in any of the recipes due to health risks.

FAN ASSISTED OVENS – reduce temperature by 20°

best results refer to manufacturers handbook.

FROZEN FOOD – make sure food has cooled completely before putting it in the freezer. **Always de-frost before cooking unless otherwise stated.** Allow plenty of time for de-frosting – I recommend taking food out of the freezer the day before it is needed and de-frosting in a cool place overnight. When completely thawed, store in the fridge until needed.

FRUIT PLATTER – I recommend serving a fruit platter with the dessert. This means that your guests have an alternative if they prefer not to eat the pudding. It takes far less time than a fruit salad, looks attractive and your guests can just help themselves with their fingers. See suggested fruit at the beginning of each season and choose three different types.

HERBS – in the recipes, I talk about handfuls. In most cases, the amount you use is a matter of taste. If you prefer to be more precise then follow the rule that 1 handful = 2 tablespoons. Use fresh herbs whenever possible, but if not, use one quarter of the quantity if using dried herbs.

MARINATING – only marinate food in non-metallic dishes. Where a recipe tells you to marinate before cooking, either do this in a non-metallic oven-proof dish or marinate in a bowl and transfer to a roasting tin before cooking.

MICROWAVES – all timings have been worked out on a 650 watt oven. When microwaving, bowls should be covered with cling-film, leaving a gap for steam to escape. As a general rule, the food being microwaved should be stirred half way through cooking.

PREPARATION OF INGREDIENTS – all recipes are quick and time saving. Unless a recipe tells you to peel a potato, tomato, etc. – don't do it – it's not necessary and just a waste of time.

QUANTITIES – there is no need to weigh everything out to the last milligram. Where possible, I talk about handfuls, tablespoons, slugs, etc. as the amount you use is a matter of taste.

SPOON MEASURES – all spoon measures are level unless otherwise stated.

HANDY HINTS

BREAD tastes so much better when served warm. This is a trick I learnt as a "Chalet Girl". Damp the bread with water, wrap in foil and put in a medium oven for 10 minutes. Even day old bread tastes and smells as if it has been freshly baked. This trick meant I could stay in bed for an extra 30 minutes instead of venturing out in the freezing cold to the bakers.

BREADCRUMBS – if you have stale bread, put it in a food processor to make breadcrumbs and store in freezer. They can be used straight from the freezer when needed.

BURNT CASSEROLES – to take the burnt taste away, add a cube of chocolate and stir in until melted – sounds strange but it works.

CHEATING – destroy any evidence of packaging of convenience foods. Read list of ingredients first though so, if anyone asks what kind of cheese you used, what is the fruit flavour in the pudding, etc. you can answer with confidence. Also, be sure to read any cooking instructions before throwing packet away.

CHOCOLATE – when melting chocolate take care as it can sometimes scorch. There are two ways of doing this: 1. Break chocolate up into a bowl and set over a saucepan of hot (not boiling) water until it melts. 2. Break chocolate up into a bowl, cover with cling-film, leaving a gap for steam to escape and microwave on medium for time mentioned in recipe or until melted. Stir half way through cooking. It is better to melt it too gradually rather than too quickly. The chocolate tends to keep its shape, so you will have to stir it with a spoon to see if it has melted enough. Chocolate melted in a microwave will go solid again quickly so you will have to use it straight away after melting.

CHOCOLATE SAUCE – where this is used, I have recommended "Smuckers" who also make good butterscotch and toffee sauces. As it is very thick it can be quite difficult to get out of the bottle but will flow more easily when warmed. Either stand the bottle on a radiator, put the bottle in a bowl of hot water or place in the microwave to warm.

CONVENIENCE INGREDIENTS – some of the convenience ingredients I have used can only be obtained from large supermarkets or specialist delis. I suggest you buy them when you see them and store for when they are needed. Certain items can be frozen, e.g. tubs of ready-made cheese or mushroom sauce, ready-rolled puff pastry, etc.

CRUSHING BISCUITS AND MERINGUE – a quick way of doing this is to transfer them to a well sealed bag, drop on the floor, and gently tread on them until crushed. Make sure the bag doesn't break open!

DRESSINGS – there are many ready-made salad dressings on the market. It is a matter of finding the one you like best but I have recommended Marks and Spencer's "Lite French Dressing" which is my favourite. It has a long shelf life so I stock up with a few bottles whenever I go to M & S.

DRESSING SALADS – with most salads it's important that they are not tossed in dressing until just before serving, otherwise they go soggy. To save time and washing up, when making your own dressing, you can mix it in the bottom of the salad bowl, put salad on top, but don't toss until the last minute.

EGGS – when separating eggs, if a bit of yolk falls into the white by mistake, the easiest way to remove it is to scoop it out with half an egg shell. The whites may not whisk stiff enough if any of the yolk remains. Always whisk egg whites first and then the yolks – this means you won't have to wash the whisk in-between. A test to see if egg whites are whisked enough, is to turn the bowl up-side-down after whisking. If they stay in the bowl they are fine, if they fall out, it means they are not whisked enough.

FILO PASTRY – so many people are put off by reading the complicated instructions on the packet. Don't – just follow my instructions. Buy fresh filo if you can, it is much easier to handle than frozen. There is no need to take it out of the fridge two hours in advance and no need to cover it with a damp tea towel (as stated in the instructions). As long as you don't leave it lying around for ages, it won't dry up. Handle it gently, but if it does rip, don't panic! Most recipes will require about four layers of filo, so make sure the ripped piece is not on the top and it won't be noticed.

FREEZING FOOD – where a recipe may be frozen, make double quantities and freeze half. This will mean that you have an instant dish when entertaining in the future.

FRESH CONVENIENCE FOODS – if you have problems finding certain fresh ingredients, e.g. fresh Napoletana sauce, fresh cheese sauce, they also come in long-life jars which will work just as well.

GELATINE – I have used powdered gelatine in all my recipes as I find it easy to handle. Always add the powder to the liquid – not the other way round. It should quickly dissolve when sprinkled on to very hot liquid in a cup and stirred. If it does not dissolve fully, this is because the liquid has cooled too soon. To rectify this, put the cup in a microwave on low for about 45 seconds or until the gelatine has melted or stand the cup in a pan of warm water over a low heat. Once the gelatine has melted, the liquid should be the same temperature as the one which you are adding it to, e.g. cool for a cold mousse and hot for a hot mousse. When I say cool, don't allow it to get completely cold, otherwise it will begin to set.

HOME-MADE – what do you do when someone asks if you made it yourself? Remember, even if you have opened the odd packet, you have still stirred it, added other ingredients, maybe cooked it, so in effect, you have made some of it yourself. Just give a smile and kind of nod. Practise in front of the mirror – you'll soon perfect the look!

LOW FAT ALTERNATIVE TO BUTTER – I recommend "Olivio" with which you can cook and it tastes good.

MISTAKES – never, ever confess if something has gone wrong. Just make a few alterations if possible and pretend that this is the way it's meant to look. For example, you burn the pastry on the filo and blueberry tarts. Just sprinkle a little extra icing sugar on so no one will realise; or the freezer fails and the orange sorbet refuses to set – this actually happened to me while working in Greece. I simply mixed it with vodka and served it before dinner as a "Screwdriver Cocktail". By the end of dinner, everyone was in such an alcoholic haze that they did not notice that they only had fruit for pudding. See more tips in individual recipes.

ONIONS WITHOUT TEARS – there are many different theories about chopping onions, including putting a metal or wooden spoon in your mouth, wearing goggles or contact lenses. I have found the only fool proof method is to light a candle and keep it near the onion – sounds strange but it really does work.

RECIPES – what to say if asked for a recipe – there are many different ways of getting round this and here are some: Say "I'll send it to you in the post" and conveniently forget. Tell them it's an old family recipe and you'll have to get permission from the family first. Say "cook's secret".

SAUCES THAT CURDLE – if the hollandaise or béarnaise sauce curdles because it has been heated too quickly, assuming you have some spare sauce, stir it in and it will stop the curdling.

THICK SAUCES – if a sauce becomes too thick – add some wine to thin it down.

VEGETABLES – if you worry about having to cook vegetables at the last minute and feel you've got to stand over the saucepan to make sure they don't go soggy, stop worrying. Here are a couple of suggestions to alleviate your worries. Cook vegetables in advance, but for slightly less time than indicated, drain and put in a non-metallic serving dish. Cover with cling-film, leaving a gap for steam to escape, and put in microwave for a few minutes before serving to heat them up. Serve straight from the microwave. The other alternative is to forget about vegetables and serve a salad instead.

ZESTING – there is quite an art to zesting so I suggest, for first timers, you buy a spare lemon to practice on. Hold the zester at an angle close to the lemon and pull down hard. Fine strips of rind should appear. I far prefer zesting the rind of fruit rather than grating it.

EQUIPMENT

Here are some items which I feel are necessary for speed and presentation:

CAKE TIN – round spring-form or loose-bottomed – approx size 24cm (9½") in diameter.

CASSEROLE – large oven-proof – at least 2.5 litres (4½ pints) in capacity.

ELECTRIC WHISK – for quickly whisking egg whites, cream, etc.

FOOD PROCESSOR – absolutely essential for short-cut cooking. Use for chopping, slicing, grating, puréeing, etc. It is incredibly time saving, especially when ingredients are processed in the right order so that you don't have to clean it out each time, e.g. chop herbs first, grate cheese second and purée vegetables third without washing it up in between. (I suggest you do before starting on the raspberry coulis though!).

GARLIC CRUSHER – the quickest way of mashing garlic. You can now buy self-cleaning ones which push the bits of garlic out from both sides.

GRATIN OR SHALLOW OVEN-PROOF DISH – 2.25 litres (4 pints) in capacity.

KEBAB STICKS – metal or wooden. If you buy metal ones, get the flat type which make turning easier. When using wooden ones, soak them in water for an hour to stop them burning.

KNIVES – you will probably already have your own favourite knives but it is very important to keep them sharp as it enables you to work more quickly and make a neater job.

LEMON SQUEEZER AND ZESTER – through zesting the skin of lemons and oranges you save yourself the pain of grating your fingers.

MICROWAVE – also extremely time saving. Can be used for de-frosting, re-heating, melting chocolate, dissolving gelatine, etc. You can also cut down on washing up by microwaving food in the dish in which it will be served.

PLATTERS – large round oval platters, either of china or glass – at least 30 cm (12") in diameter. They are always useful for arranging fruit on, serving tarts, cold main courses, etc.

PYREX BOWLS – 1 litre (1¾ pints) and other sized Pyrex bowls are useful.

RAMEKIN DISHES – at least 8. If you are buying new ones, get the ones without gold rims so that they can go in the microwave.

RING MOULD – 1 litre (1¾ pints) or 23cm (9").

ROASTING TINS – the larger the better. I would recommend vitreous enamel. They are available at good kitchen shops, some supermarkets, or by mail order from Lakeland Plastics Ltd., Alexandra Buildings, Windermere, Cumbria, LA23 1BQ.

ROULADE TINS – same as a Swiss roll tin – approx size 30cm x 22cm (12" x 8½"). I recommend vitreous enamel – it is very hard wearing and easy to clean.

SERVING BOWL – large and decorative. Useful for salads, hot vegetables, couscous, etc.

TARTLETTE TINS – vitreous enamel recommended.

TART TIN – large, loose-bottomed – approx 26cm (10½") in diameter.

TERRINE DISH – which will hold 1.5 litres (2¾ pints).

WOK – very useful when stir-frying large quantities.

USEFUL STORE CUPBOARD INGREDIENTS

You will find that you have to buy fresh ingredients every time you have a dinner party, but here are some useful items to keep in your cupboard, fridge or freezer:

Bacon-flavoured soya bits
Biscuits – amaretti, ratafia and
    brandy snap baskets
Bulgur Wheat
Chocolate – dark and white
Chocolate-coated coffee beans
Couscous
Custard – long-life in cartons
Dressings for salads – "M & S Lite
    French Dressing" recommended
Dried fruits – apricots, pears,
    prunes, sultana, raisins
Fish soup – in jars, "Select Marée"
    recommended
Flour – plain and self-raising
Fruit purées – apricot and cherry –
    "Bonne Maman" recommended
Garlic – fresh
Gelatine powder
Honey – any type
Marmalade
Mayonnaise
Meringue – ready-made in packets
Mushrooms – dried (wild) and in jars
    marinated in oil
Mustard – French and wholegrain
Noodles
Nuts – cashews, hazelnuts, pecans,
    pine, walnuts
Oils – extra virgin olive, walnut,
    hazelnut, sesame
Olive paste – black
Pepper – black peppercorns
    for grinding
Pasta – dried penne or other
    shapes
Pesto – in jars
Rice – long-grain and wild
Sea salt – ground

SAUCES:
Béarnaise sauce – in jars
Black bean sauce – "Sharwoods"
    recommended
Butterscotch sauce
Chilli sauce
Chocolate sauce
Condiverde – Mediterranean
    marinated vegetables – sold in
    jars from Sainsbury, Tesco,

other large supermarkets and
    specialist delis
Dill mustard sauce
Hollandaise sauce – in jars
Pasta sauce in jars, e.g. "Ragu",
    "Dolmio" or supermarket own
    brand – Waitrose "Pasta Sauce,
    Original Tomato" recommended
Soy sauce
Spicy tomato salsa – "Pace"
    recommended
Toffee sauce
Worcester sauce

SEEDS:
Poppy seeds
Pumpkin seeds
Sesame seeds
Stock cubes – chicken, beef, fish
    and vegetable
Sugar – brown, granulated, caster,
    icing
Sun-dried tomatoes – in oil
    and paste

TINNED:
Anchovies
Artichoke hearts
Black olives
Blackeye beans
Cannellini beans
Capers
Chopped tomatoes
Tomato purée
Vinegar – ordinary wine, balsamic

HERBS AND SPICES:
It is better to buy fresh herbs and
spices when needed but here are
some dried ones which are worth
keeping a stock of:–
Caraway seeds
Cardamom pods
Cinnamon – ground
Coriander – ground
Cumin seeds
Curry powder – mild
Dried mixed herbs
Ginger
Nutmeg

Paprika
Turmeric

ITEMS FOR THE FRIDGE:
Butter and "Olivio"
Crème fraîche
Eggs – size 2 (medium)
Fromage frais
Grated Parmesan
Milk

ITEMS FOR THE FREEZER:
Bread – ciabatta, baguette,
    other types
Fruit – raspberries and mixed
    summer fruit.
Ice cream – good quality vanilla
Orange juice – sold frozen in
    cartons
Pastry – short crust, puff and ready
    rolled puff pastry. The ready-
    rolled is usually sold fresh but
    can be kept in the freezer at
    home.

SAUCES – fresh ready-made tubs of
cheese or mushroom sauce – sold
at most large supermarkets, usually
near the fresh pasta. They can be
frozen and are handy to keep to de-
frost for emergencies.

STOCK – chicken, beef, vegetable –
sold fresh in cartons, can be kept
in the freezer at home and de-
frosted when needed.

ALCOHOL:
Baileys
Brandy
Cassis
Cointreau
Red and white wine (also handy for
the odd drink while cooking)
Sherry – dry and medium
Sickly sweet fruity liqueur which
you can buy on holiday in Spain,
Portugal, etc.
Vermouth – dry

Spring

> ## SPRING FRUIT PLATTER
> Choose three of the following fruits and arrange on a large platter.
>
> APRICOTS (dried)
> FIGS (dried)
> GRAPES (black or white) – cut into little bunches of 8-10
> KIWI – peeled and sliced or cut in quarters
> MANGO (fresh or dried)
> MELON – sliced and skin removed
> PAWPAW (papaya) – peeled, seeds removed and sliced

THE DAY BEFORE COOK

What could be more simple than coming home from work, knowing that you are expecting eight guests for dinner, and all you have to do is switch on the oven and put a few dishes in? Read on and find out more. All the following recipes can be made the day before and, apart from the stuffed chicken, can be frozen.

♀ A light Australian Chardonnay. Recommendation – Cockatoo Ridge, Chardonnay

CHEESE SOUFFLÉ WITH A CHEESE AND CHIVE SAUCE
STUFFED CHICKEN WITH MUSHROOM PÂTÉ IN FILO PARCELS
POTATOES WITH SUN-DRIED TOMATOES
RATATOUILLE WITH PESTO
MANGO SORBET WITH A PASSION FRUIT COULIS

CHEESE SOUFFLÉ WITH A CHEESE AND CHIVE SAUCE

2 tbsp grated Parmesan
oil
5 eggs
175g (6oz) Gruyère cheese – grated
1 tub (300g–350g) ready-made cheese sauce
salt and pepper
100g bag mixed salad leaves
1 tub (170g) cheese and chive dip
2 tbsp chopped chives
Oven: 190ºC, 375ºF, Gas Mark 5

Soufflés are so delicious and light to serve as a starter. Most people however wouldn't even consider it, thinking that they would have to make them at the last minute and then make their guests sprint to the table in case they sunk before they got there (the soufflés, not the guests). The beauty of this recipe is that they can actually be made in advance and can even be frozen.

Brush 8 ramekin dishes with oil and sprinkle Parmesan around the bottom and sides. Separate eggs and mix yolks with grated Gruyère cheese, cheese sauce, salt and pepper. Whisk egg whites until stiff and fold into cheese mixture. Put in ramekin dishes and cook for 20 minutes. Either serve immediately or leave to cool. As they cool they will sink but don't panic, they puff up again when re-heated.

❿ ❄ May be made up to this point the day before or may be frozen.

To re-heat – slide a knife around each soufflé, turn out on to the palm of your hand and then place on a baking tray, bottom side up. Put in oven for a further 15 minutes.

To serve – place soufflés on individual plates with some salad leaves around them and a blob of cheese and chive dip on top. Sprinkle chopped chives on top.

Cook's tip: Alternative method if you want to be a "mega cheat" – buy "Menu Fromage – Petit Soufflé" – available from some supermarkets or delis. Turn out of container onto a baking tray, bash them around to make them look home-made, cook in oven for 20 minutes and serve as above.

STUFFED CHICKEN WITH MUSHROOM PÂTÉ IN FILO PASTRY

8 chicken breasts
1 tub (approx. 110g) mushroom pâté
150g (5oz) mushrooms – chopped
1 packet fresh filo pastry or 16 sheets (measuring approx. 30cm x 18cm)
salt and pepper
olive oil
1 tub (300g–350g) ready-made mushroom sauce
Oven: 190ºC, 375ºF, Gas Mark 5

This is a recipe which will really impress the boss, girl friend, in-laws, etc.

Grease a baking tray. Cut slits in the chicken breasts lengthways and open out like a book. Spread each breast with mushroom pâté and divide half of the chopped mushrooms between them. Season, fold up and wrap in filo:–
You will need 2 sheets per breast. Lay out the first sheet and lightly brush half with oil. Fold in half to form a square and place breast on it diagonally, then fold corners in to the centre to seal. Repeat the same process with the second sheet, turning the chicken over so that the folded side is facing down and making sure that the oil is brushed between each layer. Place parcels on the baking tray, folded side down, and brush the top with oil (see page 6 for tips on using filo).

❿ May be prepared up to this point the day before, covered and refrigerated.

Cook, uncovered in oven for 45 minutes.

To make sauce add remaining chopped mushrooms to the mushroom sauce and heat as instructions on the chicken parcels.

POTATOES WITH SUN-DRIED TOMATOES

1.5kg (3lbs 5oz) large potatoes
2 medium leeks – thinly sliced
2 garlic cloves – crushed
½ jar sun-dried tomatoes (approx. 190g) – chopped
200ml crème fraîche
275ml (½pt) milk
salt and paprika
Oven:180°C, 350°F, Gas Mark 4

Similar to potatoes dauphinoise but made deliciously different by the addition of leeks and sun-dried tomatoes.

Grease an oven-proof serving dish. Scrub potatoes and slice thinly (may be done in food processor). Mix leeks, garlic and sun-dried tomatoes together. Put a third of the sliced potatoes in the dish and spread half the leek mixture on top. Repeat another third of potatoes, remaining leek mixture and finish off with the last third of potatoes. Combine crème fraîche, milk and salt and pour over potatoes. Sprinkle with paprika, cover with kitchen foil and cook for 1¾ hours. Remove foil for the last half hour for the top to brown.

◗ ❄ May be made in advance or frozen.

To re-heat – Put in oven for 30 minutes.

Cook's tips: Use the food processor to slice the leeks before slicing the potatoes. You could add grated cheese to this recipe and together with the ratatouille it would be suitable to serve for a vegetarian lunch.

RATATOUILLE WITH PESTO

2 tbsp olive oil
2 onions – peeled and sliced
2 aubergines – sliced
4 courgettes – sliced
1 red and 1 yellow pepper – cored, de-seeded and sliced
800g (2lbs) tinned chopped tomatoes
2 garlic cloves – crushed
½ jar (approx. 100g) pesto
salt and pepper

This is a vegetable ragout typical of Provencal cookery. According to the purists, the different vegetables should be cooked separately, but you can ignore that and appreciate the fact that in this recipe, everything is cooked together. It can be cooked in the microwave for convenience, even though it takes the same amount of time as cooking on top of the oven. The addition of pesto gives it a lovely rich basil flavour.

Heat oil in a large saucepan and cook onions gently for about 10 minutes until soft. Add remaining ingredients and simmer gently for 45 minutes, stirring occasionally.

Microwave method – put oil and onions in a large microwave bowl. Cover with cling film, pulling back a corner for steam to escape. Microwave on high for 7 minutes. Add remaining ingredients, cover and cook for a further 45 minutes, stirring occasionally.

◗ ❄ May be made in advance or frozen.

To re-heat – put in microwave on high for 10 minutes, stirring occasionally or re-heat gently in a saucepan for approx. 15 minutes. This quantity will serve 8-10 people.

Cook's tip: I think this tastes even better when made in advance and re-heated, so I often make double quantities and keep some in the freezer for a later date.

MANGO SORBET WITH A PASSION FRUIT COULIS

I have served this to an authentic gourmet who spent hours raving about how wonderful it was to eat real "home-made" sorbet and how you can taste the fresh mango in it!

1 litre tub mango sorbet

*1 large ripe mango or
2 small mangoes*

8 passion fruit

*large slug fruity liqueur
(approx. 4 tbsp or more) e.g.
Cointreau, Grand Marnier*

Allow sorbet to slightly soften and turn into a 1 litre pudding bowl and put in freezer until ready to serve. Peel mango, cut the flesh from either side of the stone and cut into 16 thin slices. Reserve remainder around the stone.

To make coulis – scoop out the middle of 4 passion fruit and process in a food processor or liquidizer with the remaining mango around the stone and large slug of liqueur. Pour into a jug.

◗ May be prepared up to this point the day before.

To serve – put the bowl of sorbet into a basin of hot water for a few seconds and loosen the sides with a pallet knife. Turn out onto a serving plate. (This may be done in advance and returned to the freezer.) Slice the sorbet and decorate each plate with 2 slices of mango, half a passion fruit and pour the coulis over the sorbet.

ORDER OF PREPARATION IF
MAKING IN ADVANCE:

The day before:
1. Make soufflés up to ❊
2. Prepare stuffed chicken up to ◗
3. Make potatoes up to ❊
4. Make ratatouille up to ❊
5. Prepare sorbet and coulis up to ◗

In the evening:
6. Cook chicken and heat sauce.
7. Re-heat soufflés, potatoes and ratatouille.

ORDER OF PREPARATION IN
UNDER 2 HOURS:
1. Make potatoes with sun-dried tomatoes.
2. Prepare sorbet and coulis up to ❊
3. Make soufflés up to ❊
4. Prepare chicken and cook as needed.
5. Make ratatouille.
6. Turn out soufflés and re-heat as needed.

ST. DAVID'S DAY DINNER

With leeks and lamb in this menu, what could be more suitable for a St. David's Day Dinner? Unfortunately the amaretti cheese cake is not typical of Wales but I thought it was a lot more exciting than "Welsh Cakes"!

Y *A forward fruity Bordeaux. Recommendation – Chateau Lartigue, Cotes de Castillon from France*

FEUILLETÉ OF LEEKS AU GRATIN
RACK OF LAMB WITH A SUN-DRIED TOMATO CRUST
BABY ROAST POTATOES WITH LEMON, ROSEMARY AND GARLIC
BAKED VEGETABLE PARCELS
AMARETTI, CHOCOLATE AND MASCARPONE CHEESE CAKE
WITH COFFEE ICE CREAM

FEUILLETÉ OF LEEKS AU GRATIN

Fluffy leaves of puff pastry filled with cheesy leeks.

375g packet ready-rolled puff pastry
1 egg, beaten
4 tsp sesame seeds
5 leeks – sliced
1 tub (300g–350g) ready-made cheese sauce
1 tsp grain mustard
1 glass white wine
bunch of watercress
salt and pepper
Oven: 200ºC, 400ºF, Gas Mark 6

Unroll pastry and using a cup or bowl approx 9.5cm (3¾") as a guide, cut out 8 circles. Using a sharp knife, mark the surface of the rounds with a diamond pattern. Put on a baking tray, brush with beaten egg and sprinkle sesame seeds on top. Keep in fridge until needed to cook.

Put sliced leeks into boiling water and simmer for 5 minutes. Drain well and mix with cheese sauce, mustard, white wine, salt and pepper.

◖ May be made up to this point the day before.

Put pastry in oven for 20 minutes until golden and puffed up. Meanwhile, gently heat leek mixture for about 10 minutes until hot through. Cut pastry rounds in half horizontally, place bottom half on each serving plate, divide leek mixture between them and put sesame lids on top. Garnish with watercress.

Cook's tip: Ready-rolled puff pastry can be bought from most large supermarkets and can be found in the refrigerated section. It can be frozen and I find it a handy item to keep in store for emergencies.

RACK OF LAMB WITH A SUN-DRIED TOMATO CRUST

Sun-dried tomatoes and lamb make a great combination. Buy very lean racks of lamb or trim them well yourself.

4 trimmed, lean racks of lamb
1 garlic clove – crushed
1 jar (185g) sun-dried tomato paste
salt and pepper
Oven: 200ºC, 400ºF, Gas Mark 6

Trim off any remaining fat from the lamb. Mix the crushed garlic with the sun-dried tomato paste, spread over the lamb and season.

☀ May be prepared up to this point earlier in the day.

Put on a rack over a baking tin and cook for 25–35 minutes, depending on whether you like your lamb pink or well done. Carve lamb into cutlets and serve.

Cook's tip: The lamb may be cooked on a rack over the baby roast potatoes. Some of the sun-dried tomato paste may drip though, but it will only add to the flavour of the potatoes.

BABY ROAST POTATOES WITH LEMON, ROSEMARY AND GARLIC

Not many people think of roasting new potatoes, but they are delicious and easy to cook in this way.

1.5kg (3lbs 5oz) new potatoes – scrubbed
zest and juice 1 lemon
1 handful fresh chopped rosemary
2 garlic cloves – crushed
2 tbsp olive oil
salt and pepper
Oven: 200ºC, 400ºF, Gas Mark 6

Put new potatoes in a roasting tin with all other ingredients and toss. Cook in oven for 1½ hours, tossing occasionally. The lamb may be cooked on a rack above the potatoes.

Cook's tip: To get the zest off a lemon, I prefer to use a zester rather than a grater. The art to successfully using a zester is to hold it at the correct angle to the lemon, nearly flat against it, press hard and pull down. Once you have mastered the art, you will find it incredibly simple.

BAKED VEGETABLE PARCELS

These parcels contain a mixture of baby spring vegetables. They are cooked in a foil parcel to keep in all the flavours and once made, need no attention while cooking.

1.5kg (3lbs 5oz) mixed baby vegetables – choose any four of the following: carrots, courgettes, corn, sugar snap peas, patty pans, shallots, turnips
½ can Campbell's Condensed Consommé
8 level tsp honey
salt and pepper
Oven: 200ºC, 400ºF, Gas Mark 6

Trim vegetables where necessary and if using shallots, peel and cut in half. Cut out 8 squares of foil to wrap vegetables in and pull up the sides. Divide vegetables, consommé and honey between foil squares and season. Close up the parcels, seal well and put on a baking tray.

☀ May be prepared up to this point earlier in the day.

Cook for 40 minutes. Serve in foil parcels.

Cook's tip: Patty pans are a form of baby squash, sometimes called "custard marrow" and look very pretty.

AMARETTI, CHOCOLATE AND MASCARPONE CHEESE CAKE WITH COFFEE ICE CREAM

60g (2½oz) butter

250g (9oz) amaretti biscuits

200g (7oz) dark chocolate

250g (9oz) mascarpone

250g (9oz) fromage frais

3 eggs

2 tbsp icing sugar

1 litre tub coffee ice cream

Oven: 170°C, 325°F, Gas Mark 3

Wickedly delicious – what more can I say?

Grease a round spring-form or loose-bottomed cake tin – approximately 24cm (9½") in diameter. Melt butter, crush amaretti biscuits, mix together and press into the base of the tin. Put in the fridge while you make the filling.

Break chocolate into squares and melt either in a bowl over a pan of simmering water or microwave on medium for 3-4 minutes or until melted (see Handy Hints page 6). Beat or whisk together mascarpone, fromage frais, 1 tbsp of the icing sugar and eggs. Add melted chocolate and beat well.
Pour into cake tin and cook for 45 minutes, then turn the oven off but leave cheese cake in oven for a further 15 minutes (this should prevent cracks forming). Remove from oven and allow to cool.

Allow coffee ice cream to soften slightly and then turn out into a serving bowl and return to freezer.

◖ ❋ May be made the day before or may be frozen.

To serve – loosen edges of the cheese cake and remove the sides of the tin but do not attempt to remove the base. Put on to a large serving plate and sieve remaining 1 tbsp icing sugar over the top. Slice and serve with the ice cream.

Cook's tip: For a quick way to crush amaretti biscuits – see handy hints page 6.

ORDER OF PREPARATION IF
MAKING IN ADVANCE:

The day before:
1. Make cheese cake up to ◖
2. Prepare feuilleté of leeks up to ◖

Earlier on the day:
3. Prepare lamb up to ❋
4. Prepare vegetable parcels up to ❋

In the evening:
5. Prepare potatoes and put in oven when necessary.
6. Put lamb and vegetable parcels in the oven when necessary.
7. Re-heat feuilleté and leeks ready to serve.

ORDER OF PREPARATION IN
UNDER 2 HOURS:
1. Make cheese cake.
2. Prepare potatoes and put in oven when necessary.
3. Prepare vegetable parcels and put in oven when necessary.
4. Prepare lamb and cook when needed.
5. Make starter.

EASY EXERCISE

It is recommended that the average person should take at least 20 minutes exercise a day, 3 times a week. With the hectic life-style most people lead, how do they manage to fit it in?

Well, here's one way you can entertain but still fit in the third set of tennis, 19th hole of golf or last game of Mario. Making the following recipes will be an easy exercise, especially as most of them can be prepared in advance. They are easily digestible and the iced meringue cake will boost the energy levels to prepare you for your exercise the following day.

FETA AND TZATZIKI ROULADE
FILO BASKETS WITH SALMON IN DILL HOLLANDAISE
MIXED LEAF SALAD WITH WALNUTS AND SUN-DRIED TOMATOES
NEW POTATOES IN GARLICKY OLIVE OIL
ICED MERINGUE CAKE WITH A RASPBERRY AND CASSIS COULIS

Chilean Sauvignon. Recommendation – Vina Casablanca "White Label"

FETA AND TZATZIKI ROULADE

Roulades always look impressive and make a lovely light starter. They are much easier to make than most people think.

4 eggs
175g (6oz) feta cheese – grated
100ml (5tbsp)crème fraîche
300g (11oz) tzatziki
bunch watercress
½ cucumber – sliced
8 cherry tomatoes
pepper
Oven:190ºC, 375ºF, Gas Mark 5

Grease a swiss roll tin and line with baking parchment. Separate eggs and mix yolks with grated feta, crème fraîche and pepper. Whisk egg whites until stiff and fold into feta mixture. Spread mixture evenly in the prepared swiss roll tin and cook for 15 minutes. Leave to cool. Put another piece of baking parchment on top and cover with a damp tea towel.

◐ ❋ May be prepared up to this point the day before and kept covered with a damp tea towel or may be frozen.

Turn roulade out of tin on to baking parchment. Spread tzatziki over the roulade and roll up, using baking parchment to help. Put onto a serving dish and decorate with sliced cucumber, watercress and cherry tomatoes. Cut into slices and serve with Greek olive bread or warm ciabatta, see Handy Hints page 5.

Cook's tip: If the roulade cracks when you are rolling it up, cover the crack with sliced cucumber.

FILO BASKETS WITH SALMON IN DILL HOLLANDAISE

olive oil

1 packet fresh filo pastry or 16 sheets (measuring approx. 30cm x 18cm)

1kg (2lbs 4oz) salmon fillet – skinned (ask fishmonger or supermarket to skin it for you)

1 jar (250ml) hollandaise sauce

½ jar (90g) dill sauce or dill mustard

250g (9oz) sugar snap peas

2 handfuls fresh dill

2 lemons – cut into 8 wedges

salt and pepper

Oven: 180°C, 350°F, Gas Mark 4

If you ever stop to read the instructions on a packet of filo pastry, it would scare you enough to throw it in the bin and just cook the salmon! Don't be put off – it's much easier than you think – see Handy Hints page 5. These baskets never fail to impress and once you have made one, the other seven will be "easy peasy". They are ideal for a dinner party as they can be made in advance or frozen.

To make filo baskets – you will need oven-proof bowls to mould pastry in (about 11cm / 4" in diameter). Brush the insides of the bowls with oil. Lay one sheet of filo out and brush half of it with oil and fold it in ½ to form a square. Brush top of square with oil and repeat with another sheet of filo on top – you should now have 4 layers of filo. Put inside the bowl and brush the exposed layer of filo with oil. Repeat with remaining bowls. Cook in oven for 10 minutes. When cool enough to handle, take out of the bowls and you are left with the filo baskets.

Cut salmon into chunks, top and tail sugar snap peas and cut in half. Mix salmon and sugar snap peas with hollandaise and dill sauces and season. Chop half the fresh dill and add to mixture.

☼ May be prepared up to this point earlier in the day.

◐ ❄ The filo baskets may be made the day before or frozen.

Put salmon mixture inside baskets and cook for 20 minutes. Decorate with remaining sprigs of dill and lemon wedges.

Cook's tip: Check the salmon fillets for any stray bones. An easy way to remove them is to pluck them out with tweezers.

NEW POTATOES IN GARLICKY OLIVE OIL

1.5kg (3lbs 5oz) new potatoes

1 garlic clove – crushed

1 tbsp olive oil

salt and pepper

Simple but deliciously garlicky.

Put potatoes into boiling water and simmer for 10–15 minutes. Mix crushed garlic with olive oil and pour over potatoes when cooked and drained. Season and serve.

Cook's tip: Even though I am always keen to take a short cut, garlic is one of the ingredients which I always buy fresh. All the various forms in which you can buy preserved garlic, e.g. in tubes, dried, frozen, etc. are not a patch on the real thing. If you hate washing up garlic crushers, there are some very good ones around these days which are "self cleaning". You still have to wash them up but you don't have to spend time digging out the bits that get stuck.

MIXED LEAF SALAD WITH WALNUTS AND SUN-DRIED TOMATOES

400g mixed leaves in packets

100g (3½oz) walnut halves

½ jar (190g) sun-dried tomatoes – drained and sliced

8 tbsp ready-made French dressing

I am a great fan of packets of salad leaves. They save so much time, are ready washed and give a great selection of fresh leaves. Any variety of leaves can be used for this salad.

Mix all ingredients together.

Cook's tip: Always keep the oil from the sun-dried tomatoes. It's handy for salad dressings, frying in and many other uses.

ICED MERINGUE CAKE WITH A RASPBERRY AND CASSIS COULIS

1 packet ready-made meringues (6–8 meringues)

600ml (1pt) double cream

2 tbsp icing sugar

slug of cassis or other liqueur (approx. 2 tbsp)

250g (9oz) strawberries – sliced

COULIS

250g (9oz) fresh or frozen raspberries – de-frosted

large slug cassis (approx. 4 tbsp or more)

1 tbsp icing sugar

This is an adaptation of a Pavlova, which I think you will find is far more exciting and you don't have to wait three hours for the meringue to cook.

Line a 23cm (9") tin or bowl with cling-film. Roughly crush meringues. Whisk the cream, liqueur and icing sugar together until thick. Fold in the crushed meringues and put in the cake tin or bowl. Freeze for at least 2 hours.

To make coulis – blend raspberries, cassis and icing sugar into a food processor or liquidizer. Put in a serving jug.

◑ ✳ May be prepared in advance and frozen. Keep iced meringue cake in freezer until ready to serve.

To serve – turn cake onto a serving plate and arrange sliced strawberries on top. Cut cake into slices and pour coulis over.

Cook's tip: If you are worried that "bought meringues" taste like "bought meringues" you need not. Once they are crushed up and mixed with the other ingredients, your guests will be convinced that you had to get up at 2.00am to take them out of the oven.

ORDER OF PREPARATION IF MAKING IN ADVANCE:

The day before:
1. Make roulade and keep covered with a damp tea towel.
2. Make filo baskets.
3. Make iced meringue cake and coulis.

Earlier on the day:
4. Prepare salmon up to ✳

In the evening:
5. Roll up roulade and decorate.
6. Fill filo baskets and cook when necessary.
7. Prepare potatoes and cook when necessary.

8. Prepare salad and toss in dressing before serving.
9. Slice strawberries and put on top of iced meringue cake before serving.

ORDER OF PREPARATION IN UNDER 2 HOURS:
1. Make iced meringue cake and coulis and slice strawberries.
2. Make roulade. Roll up and decorate before serving.
3. Make filo baskets. Prepare filling. Fill and cook when necessary.
4. Prepare and cook potatoes.
5. Prepare salad.

FAST FISH FEAST

I have called this menu Fast Fish Feast (or the 3 Fs) because it is incredibly fast to prepare, contains fish and is a real feast! It is perfect for a "hassle free" dinner party as it needs very little last minute attention and is incredibly easy to serve.

CROSTINI WITH MOZZARELLA, BLACK OLIVES AND ANCHOVIES
SALMON ON A BED OF COUSCOUS WITH WILD MUSHROOMS
GARLIC ROAST VEGETABLES WITH PINE NUTS
AMARETTI ICE CREAM WITH AN APRICOT COMPOTE

⚱ *Modern, rich Spanish white. Recommendation – Vinas de Gain Crianza Rioja Blanco*

CROSTINI WITH MOZZARELLA, BLACK OLIVES AND ANCHOVIES

1 loaf ciabatta bread
1 garlic clove
olive oil
350g (12oz) mozzarella
1 tin anchovies – drained
16 black olives – pitted
100g bag mixed salad leaves
6 tbsp ready-made French dressing
Oven: 190°C, 375°F, Gas Mark 5

These are made with ciabatta – a flat Italian bread. They can be eaten as a first course at the table or served with drinks (without the leaves and dressing) for people to eat in their fingers.

Cut ciabatta into 16 slices and put under grill until golden. Rub garlic clove on to one side of each slice and then brush with olive oil.

✻ May be prepared up to this point earlier in the day.

Slice mozzarella and place on top of oiled ciabatta. Cut anchovies and black olives in half and place on top of mozzarella.

Either put on a baking tray and bake in oven for 15 minutes or put under a hot grill for 3-5 minutes until the cheese is bubbling.

Arrange salad leaves around the edge of each plate and place two pieces of ciabatta in the middle. Drizzle with dressing.

Cook's tip: There are many other ingredients you can use to top these crostini, so ring the changes with tomatoes and feta, pesto and chèvre, or grilled peppers.

SALMON ON A BED OF COUSCOUS WITH WILD MUSHROOMS

1 packet (15g) dried wild mushrooms
600ml (1pt) boiling water
350g (12oz) couscous
1.5kg (3lbs 5oz) salmon fillet or 8 salmon steaks –skinned and boned
1 jar (280g) mushrooms in oil
2 tubs (300g-350g each) mushroom sauce – available from most large supermarkets
salt and pepper
2 lemons – cut into wedges
Oven: 190ºC, 375ºF, Gas Mark 5

The beauty of this is that you are combining two dishes to cook and serve together. They both add flavour to each other while cooking. I have used dried wild mushrooms which need to be soaked in boiling water to bring out their intense and concentrated flavour. The water is also used to flavour the couscous.

Put dried mushrooms into a large bowl, pour boiling water over them and leave to soak for 20 minutes. Add couscous and soak for a further 10 minutes until all the liquid has been absorbed.

Lay out 8 squares of foil and divide the couscous between them. Cut salmon into 8 (or use salmon steaks) and place on top of couscous. Finally, divide half the jar of mushrooms between the 8 salmon portions and add a little of the oil on top of each. Season and wrap up in the foil.

☀ May be prepared up to this point earlier in the day.

Place on a baking tray and cook for 20 minutes.
Add the remaining jar of mushrooms with oil to the cartons of mushroom sauce and heat as instructions on tub.
Serve the salmon and couscous parcels in the foil with a wedge of lemon. Serve the mushroom sauce separately.

Cook's tip: Instead of using the jar of mushroom in oil, you can substitute it with 200g (7oz) fresh mushrooms and a little olive oil.

GARLIC ROAST VEGETABLES WITH PINE NUTS

2 aubergines – cut into chunks
6 courgettes – sliced
6 tomatoes – cut in quarters
2 onions – cut into eighths
1 red and 1 yellow pepper – de-seeded and cut into chunks
4 garlic cloves – chopped
1 handful fresh chopped herbs – e.g. rosemary, thyme, basil
50g (2oz) pine nuts
4 tbsp olive oil
salt and pepper
Oven: 200ºC, 400ºF, Gas Mark 6

The amount of vegetables used in this recipe may look over generous, but cooked this way they are so popular that you are likely to find they will all be eaten. The components of this recipe, abundant in Santa Clara (known there as eggplant and zucchini), are now available nationally and make a vegetable dish which requires very little last minute attention.

Mix all ingredients together in a large roasting dish (you may need two) and roast in oven for 1 hour, tossing occasionally.

Cook's tip: On the off chance that you have any left over, they are delicious tossed in French dressing and eaten cold the next day.

AMARETTI ICE CREAM WITH AN APRICOT COMPOTE

1 litre tub good quality
vanilla ice cream

1 jar (600g) apricot compote –
"Bonne Maman" recommended

1 packet amaretti biscuits
(32 needed in total)

slug of Amaretto (approx 4 tbsp)
or other liqueur, e.g. Brandy,
Grand Marnier, Cointreau

I gave this recipe to a friend to make for a party and she said she had never had so many complimentary comments, even from people who said they didn't like ice cream!

Line a 1 litre terrine dish or bowl with cling-film.

Allow ice cream to soften very slightly. Crumble up 16 amaretti biscuits and mix into the ice cream with half the jar of apricot compote and the slug of liqueur. Place in prepared dish or bowl.

❇ Put in freezer for at least 2 hours.

Before serving, turn the ice cream out, slice and serve with remaining amaretti biscuits and apricot compote spooned on top.

Cook's tip: See Handy Hints page 6 on crushing biscuits.

ORDER OF PREPARATION IF
MAKING IN ADVANCE:

The day before:
1. Make amaretti ice cream.

Earlier on the day:
2. Make crostini up to ❖
3. Prepare salmon and couscous up to ❖

In the evening:
4. Finish off preparing crostini recipe
   and heat when needed.
5. Prepare roast vegetables and put in
   oven as needed.
6. Put salmon in oven and heat
   mushroom sauce.

ORDER OF PREPARATION IN
UNDER 2 HOURS:
1. Make ice cream.
2. Prepare salmon recipe and cook
   when needed.
3. Prepare roast vegetables and cook
   when needed.
4. Make crostini.

ITALY IN AN INSTANT

My first holiday abroad was to Villa Cisco on the Adriatic coast of Italy, where at the age of five, I developed a passion for Italian food. The Italians have always been renowned for good, simple cooking and it is even more popular than ever before in Britain, since the ingredients are so readily available. The following menu will give you a real taste of Italy and, together with a few glasses of Grecheto del Umbri 'Il Vignola', you'll feel able to sing an aria with Pavarotti.

*♀ A nutty Italian white.
Recommendation –
Grechetto del Umbria 'Il Vignola'*

TORTELLINI, BROCCOLI AND GORGONZOLA BAKE
BROCHETTE OF MONKFISH, PROSCIUTTO AND SAGE
GRILLED POLENTA WITH NAPOLETANA SAUCE
ROCKET, SPINACH AND WILD MUSHROOM SALAD
MASCARPONE CASSATA WITH FRESH FIGS AND AMARETTI BISCUITS

TORTELLINI, BROCCOLI AND GORGONZOLA BAKE

This is a handy pasta recipe to make for a dinner party as it can be made in advance. There are many different types of stuffed tortellini. They all work well with this recipe so choose whichever type you like the sound of best.

500g (1lb 2oz) fresh tortellini – sold in packets

250g (9oz) broccoli – remove stalks and cut into little florets

1 tub (300g–350g) ready-made cheese sauce

150g (5oz) Gorgonzola

Oven: 190ºC, 375ºF, Gas Mark 5

Put tortellini into boiling water and cook for the time stated on the packet. Add broccoli to tortellini for the last 3 minutes of the cooking time. Drain and mix with cheese sauce. Put into 8 individual little oven-proof gratin dishes or one large dish. Chop Gorgonzola and put on top.

☀ May be prepared up to this point earlier in the day.

Put in oven for 15 minutes and serve.

Cook's tip: Cook the tortellini in plenty of boiling water so that there is enough room for the broccoli to be added. You can add a few drops of oil to the water to prevent the pasta sticking together.

BROCHETTE OF MONKFISH, PROSCIUTTO AND SAGE

1.5kg (3lbs 5oz) monkfish – ask fishmonger/supermarket to remove bones and membrane

16 slices prosciutto – cut in half lengthways

1 handful fresh sage leaves

2 tbsp olive oil

2 lemons

8 kebab sticks – metal or wooden

Oven: 190ºC, 375ºF, Gas Mark 5

In Italy monkfish are called "coda di rospo" and are very popular. They have a firm and "meaty" texture and are ideal for kebabs.

Cut monkfish into 32 pieces, wrap each one in half a slice of prosciutto and thread onto kebab sticks interspersed with a sage leaf in between. Put on to a baking tray and pour over olive oil and the juice of half a lemon.

✳ May be prepared up to this point earlier in the day.

Put in the oven, uncovered, for 25 minutes, turning kebabs half way through cooking.

Cut remaining lemon into wedges and serve with kebabs.

Cook's tip: Monkfish is ideal to use in this recipe but it tends to be quite expensive. If you prefer you could use cod steaks and basil could be used instead of sage.

POLENTA WITH A NAPOLETANA SAUCE

1kg "Aurora" polenta or 1 packet powdered polenta

olive oil

grated Parmesan

1 tub or jar (approx 350g) Napoletana sauce – preferably fresh

salt and pepper

Oven: 190ºC, 375ºF, Gas Mark 5

Polenta is the name given to cornmeal in Italy. It can be bought in a powder form in packets. This needs to be cooked in water, either served as a "porridgy mush" or left to cool, sliced and grilled or baked. Alternatively, it can now be bought in the form of a large "sausage" shape, (manufactured by "Aurora" and sold at large branches of Sainsburys or specialist delis). This can be sliced and grilled or baked.

If using powdered polenta, make as instructions on packet, spread in a large oiled baking tin to a depth of about 2cm (¾") and leave to cool. Turn out of tin and with a pastry cutter (approx. 7cm [3"] in diameter) cut into 16 circles. If using "Aurora" cut into 16 rounds about 2cm (¾") thick. Brush a baking tray with oil and put polenta circles on top, brush these with oil and sprinkle with Parmesan, salt and pepper.

✳ May be prepared up to this point earlier in the day.

Either put polenta in oven for 15 minutes or under a hot grill for 4 minutes.

If you have any sage leaves left over, chop them and add to Napoletana sauce. Heat sauce according to the instructions on the container and serve with polenta.

Cook's tip: It is worth trying to find the "sausage" shaped polenta as it saves so much time.

ROCKET, SPINACH AND WILD MUSHROOM SALAD

300g (10oz) baby spinach leaves – can be bought in bags ready-washed

90g (3oz)rocket leaves

1 jar (290g) mixed wild mushrooms in oil

2 tbsp balsamic vinegar

salt and pepper

Although rocket is a relative newcomer to Britain, it has been around in Italy since ancient Roman times. This nutty, peppery flavoured leaf combines well with the spinach and mushrooms to make a really delicious salad.

Put rocket and spinach leaves in a large salad bowl. Mix mushrooms, including the oil with balsamic vinegar and season. Pour over salad before serving and toss.

Cook's tip: See Handy Hints on dressing salads page 6.

MASCARPONE CASSATA WITH FRESH FIGS AND AMARETTI BISCUITS

250g (9oz) Mascarpone

3 small pots (150g each) strawberry yoghurt

250g (9oz) packet mixed dried fruit with peel

100g (3½oz) flaked almonds

large slug (4tbsp or as much as you dare) liqueur, e.g. Marsala, Cointreau or any other fruity liqueur

8 fresh figs

8 large or 16 small amaretti biscuits

This should be served softly frozen, so you will need to take it out of the freezer to soften before serving.

Mix mascarpone, yoghurt, mixed fruit, nuts and liqueur together, put into a serving bowl and put in freezer for at least 45 minutes.

❋ May be prepared in advance and frozen. Take out of freezer 30 minutes before serving and keep in fridge.

To serve – cut figs into quarters. Spoon mascarpone cassata on to individual plates and serve with amaretti biscuits and quartered figs.

Cook's tip: The mascarpone cassata may also be put in individual ramekin dishes. If figs are not available, passion fruit, cut in half, may be used instead.

ORDER OF PREPARATION IF MAKING IN ADVANCE:

The day before:
1. Make mascarpone cassata.

Earlier on the day:
2. Prepare polenta up to ❋
3. Prepare tortellini bake up to ❋
4. Prepare brochette up to ❋

In the evening:
5. Prepare salad and toss in dressing before serving.
6. Put tortellini bake in oven.
7. Cook brochette, polenta and heat Napoletana sauce as necessary.
8. Take cassata out of freezer and into fridge.

ORDER OF PREPARATION IN UNDER 2 HOURS:
1. If using powdered polenta, prepare as instructions.
2. Make mascarpone cassata.
3. Prepare tortellini bake and put in oven as needed.
4. Prepare brochette and cook as needed.
5. Prepare polenta and sauce and cook as needed.
6. Make salad.
7. Take cassata out of freezer to soften.

LIGHT AND HEALTHY

A wonderful menu which won't overdose your guests with cholesterol – they may have to put up their pension contributions though! As so much of it can be prepared in advance, I find it an ideal menu to serve after a game of tennis with friends.

WARM MOZZARELLA, TOMATO AND BASIL TARTS
TROUT STUFFED WITH WILD RICE, MUSHROOMS AND PUMPKIN SEEDS
NEW POTATO AND RED PEPPER KEBABS
FENNEL AND CHICORY SALAD WITH A LIME DRESSING
LAYERED APPLE CRUNCH BRULÉE

♀ Chilled rosé.
Recommendation – McDowell
Grenache Rosé from California

WARM MOZZARELLA, TOMATO AND BASIL TARTS

8 thick slices brown bread – preferably granary

1 jar (190g) pesto

8 medium tomatoes – sliced

250g (9oz) mozzarella – sliced

2 handfuls fresh basil

100g bag mixed salad leaves

4 tbsp ready-made French dressing

salt and pepper

Oven: 200°C, 400°F, Gas Mark 6

The toasted bread base of these tarts gives them a wonderful crispness and also saves you the hassle of having to roll out pastry. They would also be suitable to serve as a main course for a light lunch.

Cut each slice of bread into a circle, as large as possible but avoiding the crusts, using a cup or saucer as a guide. Spread each circle with pesto, place on a baking tray and put in oven for 15 minutes.

Arrange sliced tomatoes on top of each round, followed by sliced mozzarella and half the basil, shredded. Season.

☼ May be prepared up to this point earlier in the day.

Put back in oven for 15 minutes until the cheese is bubbling.
Arrange salad leaves around the edge of each plate and drizzle with dressing.
Put the tarts in the middle and arrange remaining basil leaves on top.

Cook's tip: To shred basil leaves, just pull apart with your fingers.

TROUT STUFFED WITH WILD RICE, MUSHROOMS AND PUMPKIN SEEDS

100g (3½oz) wild rice
100g (3½oz) mushrooms – wiped and chopped
50g (2oz) pumpkin seeds
1 tbsp olive oil
8 whole trout fillets
275ml (½ pt) dry white wine
2 limes – cut into wedges
salt and pepper
Oven: 200°C, 400°F, Gas Mark 6

This makes a pleasant change from the usual trout with almonds. The crunchiness of the pumpkin seeds and wild rice give this recipe a bit of bite.

Cook wild rice according to instructions on packet (usually approximately 50 minutes). When cooked, mix with chopped mushrooms, pumpkin seeds, olive oil and season. Stuff mixture inside trout and place on a baking tray. Pour wine over.

☼ May be made up to this point earlier in the day.

Cook in oven for 20 minutes. Serve with lime wedges.

Cook's tips: Make sure you buy filleted trout – there's nothing worse than taking a mouthful of bones with the stuffing. If they are only sold on the bone, insist that your fishmonger or supermarket fillets them for you. Wild rice can be bought in a "boil in the bag" variety in some supermarkets which makes it incredibly easy to cook.

FENNEL AND CHICORY SALAD WITH A LIME DRESSING

2 bulbs fennel
2 heads chicory
200g bag mixed salad leaves
DRESSING
2 limes – zest and juice
6 tbsp olive oil
1 tsp sugar
salt and pepper

There is often confusion over chicory and endive. This is quite understandable as what we call chicory, the French call endive and vice versa. What we call chicory is the compact, pale, spear shaped plant. It has a slightly bitter taste which is delicious with the aniseed flavour of the fennel.

Trim base and any tough outer leaves off the fennel and slice together with the chicory. Put in a large salad bowl with the mixed leaves.
Make dressing by mixing all ingredients together.

Cook's tip: This salad can be prepared before your guests arrive. Put the dressing in the bottom of the bowl and the salad ingredients on top but do not toss. Cover with cling-film and toss just before serving.

NEW POTATO AND RED PEPPER KEBABS

1 kg (2lbs 4oz) new potatoes – washed
2 garlic cloves – crushed
2 tbsp olive oil
1 large or 2 small red peppers – cut into 24 chunks
salt and pepper
8 kebab s
Oven: 200°C, ᴣ ᴊ0 ℉   Ma ᴋ 6

A different, impressive and colourful way of serving new potatoes.

Put potatoes into boiling water and simmer for 12 minutes. Drain and toss in garlic and olive oil. Thread potatoes and red pepper alternately on to kebab sticks, allowing an average of 4 potatoes and 3 red pepper chunks per person.

☼ May be prepared up to this point earlier in the day.

Either put on a baking tray and put in oven for 10-15 minutes or put under a hot grill for 5-10 minutes.

Cook's tip: Wooden or metal kebab sticks ca ᵢ   ᵈ. If using wooden oᵤes, soak in water for 30 minutes before using as   ᵐ burn ᵍ.

LAYERED APPLE CRUNCH BRULÉE

A pretty healthyish pudding which creates wonderful aromas when cooking the apple with the cinnamon.

4 medium eating apples

10g (½oz) butter

2 tsp cinnamon

4 heaped tbsp brown sugar

500g (1lb 2oz) fromage frais

10 ginger nut biscuits (approx 100g [3½oz]) – crushed

Peel, core and chop apples. Melt butter in a large frying pan and add apples, cinnamon and 1 heaped tbsp brown sugar. Leave to cook gently for 5 minutes. Allow to cool slightly.

Divide apple mixture between 8 ramekins, sprinkle crushed biscuits on top, followed by fromage frais and remaining brown sugar. Put under a very hot grill until the sugar begins to bubble.

Put in fridge and allow to cool for at least 1 hour.

◑ ❊ May be made the day before or may be frozen.

Cook's tip: See Handy Hints page 6 on crushing biscuits.

ORDER OF PREPARATION IF MAKING IN ADVANCE:

The day before:
1. Make layered apple crunch brulée

Earlier on the day:
2. Prepare stuffed trout up to ❊
3. Prepare potato and red pepper kebabs up to ❊
4. Prepare starter up to ❊
5. Make dressing for salad.

In the evening:
6. Make salad but don't toss in dressing until just before serving.
7. Put tarts in oven.
8. Put trout and potato kebabs in oven.

ORDER OF PREPARATION IN 2 HOURS:
1. Make layered apple crunch brulée.
2. Cook rice for stuffed trout.
3. Prepare potato and red pepper kebabs.
4. Prepare tarts.
5. Make stuffing and prepare trout.
6. Make salad.

MEDITERRANEAN MOOD

I am sure the following tastes will bring back memories of wonderful holidays around the Mediterranean.

♀ Southern Italian white. Recommendation – Vermentino de Sardegna, Sella & Mosca

CORSICAN FISH SOUP WITH ROUILLE
CHICKEN WITH BASIL, SUN-DRIED TOMATOES AND RED PEPPER
COURGETTES WITH HERBS
PENNE WITH WALNUT PESTO
TIRAMISU

CORSICAN FISH SOUP WITH ROUILLE

3 x 780g jars French fish soup – "Select Marée" recommended or good quality tinned fish soup may be used

1 baguette – for croutons

110g (4oz) Gruyère or other hard cheese – grated

8 tbsp mayonnaise

1 tbsp tomato purée

6 garlic cloves

I tried this soup while on holiday in Corsica and was so impressed that as soon as I got home I decided to re-create it. I spent hours making fish stock out of fish heads and bones which made me and my whole house stink for days. I then discovered that you could buy wonderful jars of fish soup which are now available from most supermarkets, delis or fishmongers. I no longer smell fishy.

Thinly slice baguette and put slices under grill or in oven to brown.
To make rouille – crush 2 garlic cloves and mix with mayonnaise and tomato purée.

You will need to fill 4 small dishes with the following:– 1. croutons, 2. rouille, 3. grated cheese, 4. remaining garlic cloves peeled and cut in half.

◗ May be prepared up to this point the day before.

Tip soup into a large saucepan, gently heat until piping hot and pour into a soup tureen. Serve with the four dishes and inform your guests on how to help themselves:

take 2 croutons and rub garlic over them. Put them in a soup bowl with a blob of rouille and the grated cheese on top. Pour the soup in bowls over the croutons.

CHICKEN WITH BASIL, SUN-DRIED TOMATOES AND RED PEPPER

16 boneless chicken thighs – skin removed

2 tins (400g each) chopped tomatoes

2 tbsp tomato purée

½ jar (approx 140g) sun-dried tomatoes – drained and coarsely chopped

1 red pepper – de-seeded and sliced

2 garlic cloves – crushed or chopped

1 tsp sugar

small tin (approx 200g) black olives

2 handfuls fresh basil – shred half and keep half for decoration

salt and pepper

Oven: 190°C, 375°F, Gas Mark 5

A simple recipe with wonderful Mediterranean flavours. I prefer to use boneless thighs as they stay moist and you don't have to struggle with any bones.

Put chicken in an oven-proof dish in one layer. Mix all the other ingredients together, apart from the basil leaves for decoration, and pour over the chicken.

◗ May be prepared up to this point the day before.

Put in an oven-proof dish in one layer. Cook for 1½ hours. Decorate with basil leaves.

Cook's tip: If you're feeling kind, buy pitted olives, if not, warn your guests about the stones!

COURGETTES WITH HERBS

1kg (2lbs 4oz) courgettes

1 large onion

2tbsp olive oil

1 handful fresh chopped parsley or chives

salt and pepper

The courgettes sautéed with the herbs transform them into a really exciting vegetable.

Thickly slice courgettes and chop onion. Heat olive oil in a wok or large saucepan. Gently sauté onions, courgettes and herbs for 15 minutes, tossing occasionally. Season and serve.

Cook's tip: These will cook quite happily while you are eating your starter as they are better when served immediately after cooking while still crunchy.

PENNE WITH WALNUT PESTO

500g (1lb 2oz) penne – fresh or dried

100g (3½oz) walnut pieces – chopped

1 (190g) jar green pesto

Penne is like large tubular macaroni and can either be smooth or ridged. The walnuts introduce an interesting flavour and texture.

Cook penne as instructions on packet. Drain and return to pan with chopped walnuts and pesto. Heat through, toss and serve.

Cook's tip: Cook pasta in plenty of boiling water and add a few drops of oil to stop it sticking. This can be cooked while you are eating your starter.

TIRAMISU

300ml (½pt) double cream

2 tbsp castor sugar

250g (9oz) Mascarpone cheese

400ml (¾pt) carton ready-made custard – preferably fresh but long-life will do

slug of liqueur (approx 4 tbsp or more) – whatever you have handy, e.g. brandy, Marsala, Tia Maria

300ml (½pt) strong black coffee

200g packet Boudoirs Biscuits (Ladies Fingers)

cocoa for sprinkling

This has become a very popular dish in the past few years. It always goes down well and this recipe will show you how to make it with ease.

Whisk cream with sugar until stiff. Mix Mascarpone with custard and fold into the whipped cream.

Put slug of liqueur into the coffee and briefly dip the boudoir biscuits in but do not soak them too much otherwise they will disintegrate. Place half the boudoir biscuits in the bottom of a large serving bowl or dish followed by half the cream mixture. Repeat this with the second half of the biscuits and cream mixture. Sift cocoa on top and chill for at least 1 hour.

◗ May be made the day before.

Cook's tip: If you have any coffee with liqueur left-over, it makes a very pleasant mid-morning drink!

ORDER OF PREPARATION IF MAKING IN ADVANCE:

The day before:
1. Make tiramisu.
2. Prepare soup up to ◗. Keep croutons in an air-tight container. Rouille, grated cheese and garlic should be covered with cling-film and kept in the fridge.
3. Prepare chicken up to ◗.

In the evening:
4. Put chicken in the oven.
5. Heat soup.
6. Cook courgettes.
7. Cook pasta.

ORDER OF PREPARATION IN 2 HOURS:
1. Make tiramisu.
2. Make chicken recipe.
3. Prepare everything for fish soup.
4. Cook courgettes.
5. Cook pasta.

MEXICAN MADE EASY

I once went to Mexico for an extended holiday with my friend Judy, whose brother lives near Mexico City. Over six weeks I lost one stone – that doesn't say much for Mexican cooking. Everything was smothered in chilli and served with dried up re-fried beans. Even though I love spicy food, I found everything unbearably hot. I have adapted these recipes to make them more "Westernised" and food you will really enjoy – the only problem is, you won't lose a lot of weight in a short time.

♀ A warm ripe red. Recommendation – Casa Lapostolle, Cabernet Sauvignon

CEVICHE ☆
CHICKEN FAJITAS WITH TOMATO SALSA, CHEESE, SOUR CREAM AND CHIVES
SPICY MIXED BEAN SALAD
GREEN LEAF SALAD WITH A GUACAMOLE DRESSING
TEQUILA SUNRISE SURPRISE

CEVICHE ☆

This is raw marinated fish – it may not sound tasty to you but is actually delicious! You can use many different kinds of fish for this recipe.

700g (1½lbs) salmon, mackerel, halibut, haddock, tuna or monkfish

1 onion – thinly sliced

4 tomatoes – roughly chopped

juice of 4 lemons or 6 limes

3 tbsp olive oil

1 handful fresh chopped parsley

salt and pepper

Cut fish into strips and mix in a bowl with all other ingredients except parsley. Cover with cling-film and leave to marinate for at least 4 hours.

◗ May be prepared up to this point the day before.

Mix with chopped parsley and serve with warm crusty bread (see Handy Hints page 5.)

Cooks tip: You can tell when the fish is ready to eat as it changes colour and looks as if it has been cooked.

CHICKEN FAJITAS

16–24 large flour tortillas

8 skinless, boneless chicken breasts – cut into strips

2 onions – sliced

1 green, 1 yellow and 1 red pepper – de-seeded and sliced

1 jar (150g) Stir-fry Black Bean Sauce – "Sharwoods" recommended

2 tbsp oil

1 jar mild tomato salsa – "Pace" recommended

2 tomatoes – chopped

200ml crème fraîche or sour cream

bunch chives – chopped

110g (4oz) cheese (any kind)–grated

salt and pepper

Oven: 220ºC, 425ºF, Gas Mark 7

Fajitas (pronounced far-hee-tahs) is a classic northern Mexican dish. They are soft flour tortillas filled with grilled meat, poultry or fish. I have used chicken in this recipe and cooked it in the oven. I have cooked it this way as it needs very little attention, rather than the more traditional way of grilling or frying which needs constant watching.

Mix together chicken, onions, peppers, black bean sauce, oil, salt and pepper. Put into an oven-proof serving dish and allow to marinate for at least 30 minutes.

You will need 3 small serving bowls. Mix salsa with chopped tomatoes to put in one bowl, mix crème fraîche or sour cream with chives to put in another and put grated cheese in the third.

☼ May be prepared up to this point earlier in the day.

Put chicken in oven, uncovered for 40 minutes, tossing half way through. To warm tortillas, put in microwave (in batches of 8 at a time as needed) on high for 40 seconds or following instruction on packet.

To serve – put everything on the table for your guests to help themselves. They should take a tortilla, put some chicken mixture on top, add a blob from each of the three dishes, then roll up the tortilla like a cigar.

Cook's tip: The great thing about fajitas, is that everyone gets to assemble their own. Provide plenty of napkins – this can be messy!

GREEN LEAF SALAD WITH GUACAMOLE DRESSING

400g bag mixed green leaves

1 tub ready-made guacamole

4 tbsp ready-made French dressing

This creamy, spicy dressing adds a new dimension to green leaves.

Mix guacamole with French dressing and toss over salad leaves.

Cook's tip: If you can't find ready-made guacamole, mash a ripe avocado with a fork, mix with ½ tsp chilli powder and then add to the French dressing.

SPICY BEAN SALAD

300g (11oz) French beans

2 tins (400g each) mixed bean salad – drained

1 tin (400g) broad beans – drained

2 red chillies – de-seeded and finely chopped or a few drops of chilli sauce

8 spring onions – chopped

1 handful fresh chopped coriander

6 tbsp ready-made French dressing

salt and pepper

Now that you can buy tinned mixed beans, it makes this recipe so much easier than having to buy hundreds of different types of dried bean, soaking them overnight and boiling them the next day. Opening a tin is much easier.

Top and tail French beans and cook in boiling water for 10 minutes. Drain and put in a large salad bowl with all remaining ingredients.

☼ May be made earlier in the day.

TEQUILA SUNRISE SURPRISE

500ml tub lemon sorbet

500ml tub orange sorbet

COULIS

250g (9oz) fresh or frozen
raspberries – de-frosted

2 tbsp icing sugar

large slug tequila – as much as you
dare – other alcohol may be used
instead, e.g. rum, brandy, sherry

A real tequila sunrise is a cocktail made with tequila, orange juice and grenadine. The surprise is, that you won't be getting this. This recipe is a bastardised dessert using a two-tone sorbet and an alcoholic raspberry coulis.

Allow lemon sorbet to soften slightly and spread into a 1 litre bowl. Return to freezer for 1 hour or until firm. Repeat process with orange sorbet, spreading gently to avoid disturbing the lemon sorbet. Cover with cling-film and return to freezer for at least 1 hour.

Blend raspberries in a food processor or liquidizer with icing sugar and tequila to make a coulis.

◐ ❊ May be prepared up to this point the day before. The sorbet and the coulis can be kept in the freezer for one month. Defrost coulis and serve chilled.

To serve – Put the bowl of sorbet into a basin of hot water for a few seconds and loosen the sides with a palate knife. Turn on to a serving plate (this may be done in advance and returned to the freezer until ready to serve). Slice the sorbet and serve with raspberry coulis.

Cook's tips: Other types of sorbets may be used as long as they are contrasting colours, e.g. mango with blackcurrant. Pour yourself a tequila sunrise cocktail while you're making this.

ORDER OF PREPARATION IF
MAKING IN ADVANCE:

The day before:
1. Make ceviche.
2. Make tequila sunrise surprise.

Earlier on the day:
3. Prepare fajitas up to ❊
4. Make spicy bean salad.

In the evening:
5. Prepare green leaf salad and dress before serving.
6. Put chicken in oven as necessary.
7. Warm bread in oven.

ORDER OF PREPARATION IN 2 HOURS
1. Make ceviche ☆
2. Make tequila sunrise surprise.
3. Prepare fajitas and cook as necessary.
4. Make bean salad.
5. Prepare green salad and toss before serving.

A TOUCH OF THE ORIENT

Have you always thought that Oriental cooking meant hours of preparation followed by last minute sweating over a wok? This is exactly what I used to think until I started working on Oriental recipes which can be prepared quickly, in advance and don't need cooking at the last minute.

CRAB, SWEETCORN AND GINGER SOUP WITH CRISPY SEAWEED AND PRAWN CRACKERS

OVEN BAKED TIGER PRAWNS IN A BLACK BEAN SAUCE

SESAMIED EGG NOODLES

POPPADOM BASKETS WITH AN ORIENTAL SALAD AND PEANUT DRESSING

HOT MANGO SOUFFLÉS WITH A KUMQUAT AND COINTREAU SAUCE

♀ A spicy white. Recommendation – Vina Casablanca, Gewurztraminer, Casablanca Valley from Chile

CRAB, SWEETCORN AND GINGER SOUP WITH CRISPY SEAWEED AND PRAWN CRACKERS

The ginger gives this soup a wonderful flavour – it must be fresh to achieve this effect.

3cm (1¼") cube fresh root ginger – peeled
2 tins (325g each) sweetcorn – drained
4 tbsp dry sherry
2 tins (170g each) crab – or flesh of 2 fresh crabs
1.5 litres (2½ pts) chicken or fish stock (made with 2 chicken or fish stock cubes and boiling water)
1 packet (40g) crispy seaweed (if you cannot find this use chopped coriander instead)
2 packets prawn crackers
salt and pepper

Put ginger in a food processor or liquidizer to chop. Add sweetcorn and sherry and process to a pulp. Take out of processor and mix with crab meat.

☼ May be prepared up to this point earlier in the day.

Put crab mixture into a large saucepan with hot stock and heat gently until piping hot.

Cook seaweed as instructions on packet.

To serve – pour soup into bowls, sprinkle seaweed / coriander on top and serve with prawn crackers.

Cook's tip: Prawn toasts go wonderfully with the soup. Unfortunately they cannot be made in a "dash" and are only available at a few shops. If you do come across them, buy them and use instead of the prawn crackers.

CRAB AND CORIANDER FISH CAKES WITH A SPICY TOMATO SALSA

8 small dressed crabs in shells

8 spring onions – thinly sliced
(reserve 2 tbsp for salsa)

1 handful fresh chopped coriander

2 tsp cumin seeds

4 tbsp mayonnaise

3 eggs – beaten

110g (4oz) breadcrumbs (made
from 4 slices brown bread) – see
Handy Hints page 5

oil or butter – for greasing baking tray

2 lemons – cut into 8 wedges

salt and pepper

SPICY TOMATO SALSA

1 jar (approx. 225g) mild salsa
– "Pace" recommended

2 tomatoes – chopped

reserved 2 tbsp spring onions

Oven: 220ºC, 425ºF, Gas Mark 7

This fish cake recipe is ideal for a dinner party as it can be prepared in advance and then baked in the oven. It is important to buy the crabs in their shells as the shells are used in the potato recipe.

Grease a baking tray. Remove crab meat from shell, but retain shell for potatoes. Put crab into a large bowl with all other ingredients, except the lemons, and mix together. Form into 16 round cakes and put onto the baking tray.

To make salsa – mix jar with chopped tomatoes and reserved spring onions.

◗ May be made up to this point the day before.

Cook fish cakes in oven for 20 minutes and serve with tomato salsa and lemon wedges.

Cook's tip: You will need to form the fish cakes in your hands, so you might as well mix the ingredients together with them as well.

STIR-FRIED SESAME CABBAGE

2 tbsp sesame oil

4 tbsp sesame seeds

1 large white cabbage

4 tbsp soy sauce

2 tbsp dry sherry

The sesame seeds and other ingredients in this recipe transform a rather boring vegetable into something really exciting. The cabbage takes on the other flavours, giving it a wonderful nutty taste.

Cut cabbage into quarters, remove core and dice thickly. Heat a wok or large frying pan and add sesame oil. When smoking, add sesame seeds and cabbage and allow to cook over a high heat for 2 minutes, stirring frequently. Add soy sauce and sherry and continue cooking until cabbage begins to soften slightly – approximately 5 minutes. Serve immediately.

Cook's tip: This needs to be cooked just before serving. I suggest you slip into the kitchen after the first course and quickly stir-fry – it will only take a few minutes. It looks good served straight from the wok.

POTATOES EN COQUILLES

8 crab shells

3 packets "Potato Sauté with
Onion and Bacon"

1 handful fresh, chopped parsley

Oven: 220ºC, 425ºF, Gas Mark 7

"En Coquilles" means in a shell and this recipe, which only involves opening three packets, is made special by serving them in the crab shells. This is guaranteed to impress.

Wash crab shells. Divide the potato mixture between shells and put on a baking t

☼ May be prepared earlier in the day.

Cook in oven for 40 minutes. Sprinkle with chopped parsley and serve.

Cook's tip: These packets of potatoes are long-life and are a very useful store cupboard ingredient to use at the last minute.

OVEN BAKED TIGER PRAWNS IN A BLACK BEAN SAUCE

900g (2lbs) uncooked, shelled tiger or king prawn tails – fresh or frozen (if you cannot find uncooked prawns, then the cooked ones will do)

2 red peppers – de-seeded and thinly sliced

3 leeks – thinly sliced

2 bottles (150g each) Stir-fry Black Bean Sauce – "Sharwoods" recommended

4 tbsp soy sauce

2 handfuls fresh chopped coriander

Oven: 190ºC, 375ºF, Gas Mark 5

These days you can achieve real Oriental flavours without having to go to China to buy your ingredients.

If using frozen prawns, de-frost first. Mix all ingredients together, except half the coriander, and put in an oven-proof dish. Cover and leave to marinate for at least 30 minutes.

☼ May be prepared up to this point earlier in the day.

Put in oven, covered with foil, and cook for 40 minutes, tossing half way through. Serve on a bed of sesamied noodles and sprinkle with remaining chopped coriander.

Cook's tip: The same cooking time applies to cooked or uncooked prawns. Uncooked prawns are a greyish colour and turn pink when cooked. They give a slightly better flavour to this dish but if you can't find them, the cooked ones will be fine to use instead.

SESAMIED EGG NOODLES

2 packets (250g each) thread egg noodles

2 tbsp sesame oil (other oil will do but will not give the noodles such a good taste)

4 tbsp sesame seeds

salt and pepper

Noodles come in many shapes and sizes. The thin "thread" noodles go well with this recipe but other types may be used instead.

Cook noodles as instructions on packet. Drain, toss in sesame oil and seeds and season.

☼ May be cooked earlier in the day and re-heated in a microwave on high for 5-7 minutes, tossing half way through.

You may need to add more sesame oil if the noodles are sticking.

Cook's tip: Left-over noodles are good to throw into soups.

POPPADOM BASKETS WITH AN ORIENTAL SALAD

8 poppadoms – plain or spicy

1 Chinese cabbage – shredded

150g (5oz) bean sprouts

8 spring onions – sliced diagonally

DRESSING

8 tbsp sesame oil (or olive oil)

1 tbsp vinegar

1 tsp soy sauce

2 tbsp crunchy peanut butter

salt and pepper

So easy but guaranteed to impress your friends.

You will have to make the poppadom baskets one at a time in a microwave. Place a poppadom over a ramekin or empty jam jar turned upside down and microwave on high for 45 seconds to 1 minute.

Make dressing by mixing all ingredients together – can be done in a jar and given a good shake.

◑ May be prepared up to this point the day before.

Put Chinese cabbage, bean sprouts and sliced spring onions in a bowl and toss in dressing. Put into poppadom baskets.

Cook's tip: If you can't be bothered to make the dressing, add some peanuts to the salad and use a bought ready-made dressing.

GRATIN OF PEARS

8 pears

juice of 1 lemon

400ml crème fraîche

2 tbsp fruity liqueur, e.g. Poire William, Kirsch, Cointreau, Grand Marnier

4 heaped tbsp brown sugar

Oven: 190°C, 375°F, Gas Mark 5

There are many different varieties of pear but any type can be used for this recipe. It doesn't matter if they are not very ripe as they will soften when cooking.

Cut pears in half, scoop out core with a teaspoon and peel. Lay in a large gratin or oven-proof dish in one layer, flat side down. Sprinkle with lemon juice. Mix crème fraîche with liqueur and pour on top of pears. Sprinkle brown sugar on top.

✦ May be prepared up to this point earlier in the day.

Cook in oven for 30 minutes and serve.

Cook's tip: If you go to France, bring back some Poire William or Kirsch. They go very well in this recipe and are also pleasant to drink on a cold winters day.

ORDER OF PREPARATION IF MAKING IN ADVANCE:

The day before:
1. Make the crab fish cakes and salsa up to ◖

Earlier on the day:
2. Prepare bread twists and make dressing for the salad.
3. Prepare potatoes up to ✦
4. Prepare pears up to ✦

In the evening:
5. Make starter and cook bread twists when needed.
6. Put crab cakes and potatoes in oven as needed.
7. Prepare cabbage and stir-fry before serving.
8. Put pears in oven while eating main course.

ORDER OF PREPARATION IN UNDER 2 HOURS:
1. Prepare pears au gratin and cook while eating main course.
2. Prepare crab cakes and salsa and cook as needed.
3. Prepare potatoes and cook as needed.
4. Prepare cabbage and stir-fry before serving.
5. Make bread twists.
6. Prepare starter.

THE POPE'S PARADISE

I f it's fish it must be Friday and what could impress the Pope more than monkfish?

♀ *A nutty Italian white.*
Recommendation – Greco di Puglia

BAKED CHÈVRE WITH PESTO
ROAST MONKFISH WITH A COULIS OF RED AND YELLOW PEPPERS
HARICOT VERTS WITH PINE NUTS
MINTED NEW POTATOES
CHOCOLATE SQUARES OF ST. PETER WITH A
FEATHERED CHOCOLATE CRÈME ANGLAISE

BAKED CHÈVRE WITH PESTO

1 loaf French bread
4 individual rounds or a 400g (14oz) log of chèvre
½ jar (approx. 85g) red or green pesto
100g bag mixed salad leaves
4 kiwi fruit
8 tbsp ready-made French dressing
Oven: 190ºC, 375ºF, Gas Mark 5

People who think they don't like chèvre (goat's cheese) usually change their mind when it is baked as it takes on a different consistency and taste.

Slice French bread into 16 thin slices. Brown under grill on both sides and place on a baking tray. Cut each chèvre in half to form two thin rounds and then in half again across the middle (or cut log into 8 thin rounds and then in half across the middle). Spread pesto thinly on each piece of toasted French bread and put a piece of chèvre on top.

☀ May be prepared up to this point earlier in the day.

Peel and slice kiwi and arrange with salad leaves around the edge of each plate. Put bread with chèvre in oven for 10-15 minutes until it begins to get "gungy". Place two pieces of French bread in the middle of each plate and drizzle with French dressing.

Cook's tips: If you rub a knife with oil, it prevents the chèvre sticking to it and makes it easier to cut. This recipe is also ideal as a light lunch dish.

Opposite: St David's Day Dinner
(page 13)

MONKFISH WITH A COULIS OF RED AND YELLOW PEPPERS

1.5kg (3lbs 5oz) monkfish – ask for bones and membrane to be removed
6 garlic cloves
juice of 1 lemon
2 tbsp olive oil
2 red peppers
2 yellow peppers
1 onion – cut into quarters
275ml (½pt) fish stock (made from 1 fish stock cube and boiling water)
salt and pepper
Oven: 220ºC, 425ºF, Gas Mark 7

Monkfish have incredibly ugly, ferocious looking faces. Fortunately, the head is usually removed before being put on display, otherwise no one would buy them. What they lack in beauty, they make up for in flavour and texture.

Cut monkfish into 8 pieces. Crush two garlic cloves and mix with lemon juice, olive oil, salt and pepper. Pour over monkfish and leave in marinade for at least 1 hour.

To make coulis – cut peppers in half and de-seed. Place in a roasting dish, cut side down, with remaining four cloves garlic, onion and fish stock. Cook in oven for 40 minutes. Put the yellow peppers with half the stock, garlic and onion into a food processor until smooth. Repeat process with red peppers.

◖ May be prepared up to this point the day before.

Transfer monkfish to a roasting dish and cook in marinade for 20 minutes, basting half way through. Heat coulis separately, either in a microwave for two minutes each or in saucepans over a gentle heat.

To serve – put monkfish on plates and pour red coulis on one side of fish and yellow coulis the other.

Cook's tip: To save washing up, blend the yellow peppers first, scrape out as much as you can from the processor, then blend the red peppers – any yellow left behind won't show.

HARICOT VERTS WITH PINE NUTS

1kg (2lbs 4oz) French beans
4 tbsp – approx 50g (2oz) pine nuts
1 tin (400g) chopped tomatoes – drained
salt and pepper

These beans provide a lovely combination of colours and textures.

Top and tail beans and cook in boiling water for 7 minutes or until just tender. Drain and return to pan with pine nuts, tomatoes, salt and pepper and allow to heat through for a couple of minutes.

Cook's tip: If you are in a real rush, you can buy beans already topped and tailed.

MINTED NEW POTATOES

1.5kg (3lbs 5oz) new potatoes
25g (1oz) butter or "Olivio"
1 handful fresh chopped mint
salt and pepper

There are many different types of mint, e.g. peppermint, spearmint, apple mint, lemon mint, and any of these can be used in this recipe. The mint gives these potatoes a lovely fresh taste.

Put potatoes into boiling water and simmer for 10-15 minutes. Drain and toss with butter or "Olivio", chopped mint and season.

Cook's tip: Instead of fresh mint, you can use a tablespoon of mint jelly.

Oppᵉ   A
(pᵃ

CHOCOLATE SQUARES OF ST. PETER WITH A FEATHERED CHOCOLATE CRÈME ANGLAISE

1 packet "Betty Crocker" brownie mix

400g carton ready-made custard – preferably fresh but long-life will do

125ml (4fl oz) milk

bottle of chocolate sauce

This looks so impressive that your guests would "freak" if they knew how easy it is. Just sit back and enjoy all the compliments. Make brownies according to instructions on packet but cook for 5 minutes less than indicated. Leave to cool and cut into 12 squares (you will have 4 extra).

◗ ❋ The brownies may be made the day before or may be frozen.

Make Crème Anglaise by mixing custard with milk and heat according to instructions on custard carton. Warm brownies either in microwave on medium for 2 minutes or cover with foil and put in oven for 10 minutes.

To serve – pour Crème Anglaise on to each plate and put a brownie in the middle. Trickle a line of chocolate sauce in a circle around the brownie. With the point of a knife, draw out the chocolate sauce at intervals into the Crème Anglaise to form a feathered affect. This recipe is enough for 12 people.

ORDER OF PREPARATION IF MAKING IN ADVANCE:

The day before:
1. Prepare monkfish and coulis up to ◗
2. Prepare chocolate squares up to ❋

Earlier in the day:
3. Prepare chèvre starter up to ❋
4. Prepare potatoes and cook as necessary.
5. Prepare haricot verts and cook as necessary.
6. Cook fish and heat coulis.
7. Heat pudding when needed.

ORDER OF PREPARATION IN UNDER 2 HOURS:

1. Marinate monkfish and make coulis – cook monkfish as necessary.
2. Make chocolate squares and Crème Anglaise and warm before serving.
3. Prepare and cook potatoes.
4. Prepare and cook haricot verts.
5. Make starter.

THE ALRESFORD PARTY

I have named this menu "The Alresford Party" because every time I eat watercress mousse, I think of Alresford, in Hampshire, where watercress abounds. It grows in free flowing streams and this menu conjures up images of wonderful long lunch and dinner parties eaten outside on warm summer days. It can also be served as a buffet with the salmon either hot or cold.

WATERCRESS MOUSSE WITH A TOMATO AND BASIL SALSA
LAYERED SALMON, SPINACH AND MUSHROOM IN A PUFF PASTRY ENVELOPE WITH LEMON HOLLANDAISE
NEW POTATOES WITH ANCHOVIES
THE EVELYN FRENCH BEAN AND BABY CORN SALAD
GIANT CHOCOLATE SHELL FILLED WITH BROWN BREAD ICE CREAM

♀ A crisp aromatic Sauvignon Blanc. Recommendation – Montana Sauvignon Blanc from New Zealand

WATERCRESS MOUSSE WITH A TOMATO AND BASIL SALSA

A lovely light refreshing mousse for a hot summers day.

Brush a 23cm (9") ring mould or bowl with oil. Heat 4 tbsp of the stock to boiling point, sprinkle gelatine on top and stir until dissolved.

Leave to cool.

Put all other mousse ingredients (except half a bunch of watercress and the cherry tomatoes) into a food processor until smooth. Add cooled gelatine and pour into ring mould. Put in fridge for at least 2 hours.

To make salsa – mix all ingredients together.

◗ May be made up to this point the day before.

To serve – loosen edges of mousse with a palate knife and turn out onto a serving plate. Decorate with remaining watercress and cherry tomatoes.

Serve with salsa and warm bread – see Handy Hints page 5.

Cook's tips: This mousse looks especially impressive made in a ring mould but can also be made in a bowl or terrine dish. See Handy Hints page 6. for tips on gelatine.

oil for brushing
1 carton (284ml/½pt) ready-made chicken or vegetable stock
1 sachet (11g) gelatine
3 bunches watercress (approx 75g each)
250g (9oz) fromage frais – the low fat variety may be used
4 heaped tbsp mayonnaise
16 cherry tomatoes
salt and pepper
TOMATO AND BASIL SALSA
1 tin (400g) chopped tomatoes – drained
8 spring onions – thinly sliced
1 garlic clove – crushed
1 tbsp balsamic vinegar
1 handful chopped basil
1 tsp sugar
salt and pepper

LAYERED SALMON, SPINACH AND MUSHROOM IN A PUFF PASTRY ENVELOPE WITH LEMON HOLLANDAISE

2 packets (375g each) ready-rolled puff pastry
2 salmon fillets each weighing approx 500g (1lb 2oz)
500g (1lb 2oz) frozen leaf spinach – de-frosted and drained
110g (4oz) mushrooms – sliced
100ml crème fraîche
1 egg – beaten
1 jar (250ml) hollandaise
zest and juice of 1 lemon
salt and pepper
Oven: 190ºC, 375ºF, Gas Mark 5

You can't fail to impress with this recipe. It may sound slightly complicated, but after you have made it once, you'll be making it again and again with your eyes closed.

Cut a third off each piece of puff pastry and roll into two rectangles – slightly larger than each salmon fillet. Put on a greased baking tray and cook for 15 minutes. Allow to cool.

Put a salmon fillet on top of each cooked pastry rectangle, followed by the spinach, mushrooms, crème fraîche, salt and pepper. Thinly roll out the two remaining pieces of pastry, making each one large enough to go over the fish. Trim off untidy edges and keep for decoration. Brush beaten egg around the edge of each piece of pastry and put on top of fish, tucking the sides under the base. Brush top with beaten egg. Use left-over trimmings for decoration and brush with egg.

☀ May be made up to this point earlier in the day.

Cook for 30 minutes.

Lemon hollandaise – mix zest and juice of lemon with hollandaise sauce. Put in a bowl covered with cling-film, with a gap for steam to escape, and microwave on low for 2 minutes. Alternatively stand bowl in very hot water for 5 minutes. The salmon envelopes and hollandaise may be served hot or cold.

◖ If serving cold, the salmon envelopes may be cooked the day before and kept in the fridge overnight.

Cook's tips: This recipe is more simple to make for 10-12 using whole salmon fillets. It is worth making this quantity even if you are only cooking for 8 as you can eat it cold the next day and save having to cook. Heat the hollandaise gradually otherwise it may curdle. It is better to serve it just warm rather than risk over-heating.

NEW POTATOES WITH ANCHOVIES

1.5kg (3lbs 5oz) new potatoes
1 tin anchovies in olive oil – chopped with oil reserved
1 handful chopped parsley
1 tbsp balsamic vinegar

An unusual way of serving potatoes which can be eaten hot or cold.

Scrub potatoes and cook in boiling water for about 15 minutes or until tender. Toss in remaining ingredients and serve.

☀ If serving cold, may be prepared earlier in the day.

Cook's tip: As the anchovies are salty, do not add any extra sa

THE EVELYN FRENCH BEAN AND BABY CORN SALAD

300g (11oz) French beans – topped and tailed

250g (9oz) baby sweetcorn

1 cos or 2 baby gem lettuces

8 tbsp ready-made French dressing

Baby corn is corn-on-the-cob which is harvested when immature. Together with the French beans they make a lovely colourful salad which is so simple to make.

Put French beans and baby corn into boiling water and allow to simmer for 7 minutes. Drain, toss in dressing while still hot and season. Leave to cool.

☀ May be prepared up to this point earlier in the day.

To serve – shred cos or gem lettuce and mix with French beans and corn.

GIANT CHOCOLATE SHELL WITH BROWN BREAD ICE CREAM

300g (11oz) dark chocolate

40g (1½oz) butter

100g (3½oz) brown breadcrumbs (made by putting 4 slices bread in a food processor)

3 heaped tbsp brown sugar

1 litre vanilla ice cream

slug liqueur (approx 4 tbsp) e.g. brandy, port, rum or any cheap liqueur you want to get rid of!

Yet another recipe to impress. The chocolate shell is so simple to make but will leave your guests thinking you have spent hours creating this magnificent sculpture.

Line a bowl, approximately 20cm (8") in diameter, with foil and smooth down. Melt the chocolate with 2 tbsp water – either in a bowl over a pan of simmering water until melted or microwave in a bowl on medium power for 4 minutes or until melted. Add butter, cut into little pieces, and stir until smooth. Put into the lined bowl and, using the back of a spoon, gently spread over base and up sides. Chill until solid.

To unmould – lift the chocolate shell out of the bowl holding the foil, then carefully peel off the foil. Return to fridge.

To make ice cream – mix breadcrumbs with sugar and put in a baking tray under a hot grill, tossing frequently, for 5-7 minutes until toasted. Leave to cool. Allow vanilla ice cream to slightly soften and mix in toasted breadcrumbs and liqueur. Freeze for at least 2 hours and store in the freezer until ready to serve.

◑ All the above may be made in advance. The chocolate shell will keep in a fridge for up to 5 days.

To serve – allow chocolate shell to stand at room temperature for 1-2 hours. Scoop ice cream into shell.

Cook's tips: If you are really pushed for time buy a good quality brown bread ice cream instead.

ORDER OF PREPARATION IF MAKING IN ADVANCE:

The day before:
Knowing salmon and salsa.
If serving salmon cold, make salmon envelopes up to ◑
salmon hollandaise sauce and brown

Earlier on the day:
4. Make French bean salad up to ☀
5. If serving potatoes cold, cook in morning.
6. If serving salmon hot, prepare up to ☀

In the evening:
7. If serving hot, cook salmon and potatoes as necessary.
8. Turn out mousse.

ORDER OF PREPARATION IN UNDER 2 HOURS:

1. Make watercress mousse and salsa.
2. Make ice cream and chocolate shell. Prepare salmon envelopes and salmon hollandaise and cook as necessary.
3. Make french bean salad.
4. Prepare potatoes and cook.

THE ASCOT PICNIC

Many people who have come to see me demonstrate this menu have told me that they have used it for elegant picnics and summer parties and really impressed their friends. It's a moveable feast so next time you go to Ascot, Henley or Glyndebourne you'll know what to take. On the other hand, don't wait for a special event – just organise a lakeside or parkside picnic as an excuse to show off your culinary skills (it's equally good eaten in the back garden.)

MARINATED OLIVES AND FETA ☆
CROUSTADES WITH EGG MOUSSE AND MOCK CAVIAR
SALAD OF LAMB FILLET WITH MINT AND CORIANDER ☆
WATERCRESS, ROCKET AND BABY TOMATO SALAD
COUSCOUS WITH PINE NUTS AND MARINATED VEGETABLES
BLUEBERRY FILO TARTS

*♀ Chilled Beaujolais.
Recommendation – Beaujolais village, Domaine St Enemond from France*

MARINATED OLIVES AND FETA ☆

This can be made weeks ahead and is ideal to nibble with drinks. It also makes a lovely present to take to a dinner party instead of boring old chocolates.

200g (7oz) feta cheese
350g (12oz) black olives
2 garlic cloves – crushed
1 heaped tbsp dried mixed herbs
600ml (1pt) olive oil

Cut feta into cubes (approx 1.5 cm / ½") and mix with all other ingredients. Put in an air-tight jar and top up with olive oil if necessary. Preferably, leave to marinate for 2 days. Once jar is opened, store in a fridge. Will keep for up to one month.

Cook's tip: I often keep a spare jar of this as it's so handy to serve if someone pops in for a drink. If you keep it in the fridge, allow it to stand at room temperature for about half an hour as the olive oil becomes solid when cold. Alternatively, you can put it in the microwave on de-frost until oil is runny.

CROUSTADES WITH EGG MOUSSE AND MOCK CAVIAR

This is one of my husband's favourites, but I w n't t   d when he described it as an "up-market egg m c   h"!

12 medium slices brown bread
olive oil
3 eggs – hard boiled
3 heaped tbsp mayonnaise
small jar lumpfish caviar (black or red)
salt and pepper
Oven: 200ºC, 400ºF, Gas Mark 6

Using a round pastry cutter, cut two circles of bread ou   cn   ce.   on a baking tray, brush with oil and bake in oven for 15 minut

Shell eggs and put in a food processor wi   aise, smooth.

● The croustades may be made a few d   bef   d k   container and the egg mousse   made   fo

Spread a heaped teaspoon of egg mousse on each croustade and put a blob of caviar on top. This recipe makes 24.

Cook's tip: This is ideal to serve with drinks – no need for plates and you can save washing up.

SALAD OF LAMB FILLET WITH MINT AND CORIANDER ☆

This salad has the most wonderful combination of flavours and looks so colourful with the apricots and grapes.

Remove any fat from lamb, thinly slice and cut into strips. Put into a large bowl and mix with chopped coriander, chopped mint (reserve leaves for decoration), mint jelly, yoghurt, salt and pepper.

◑ May be made up to this point earlier in the day or the day before.

To serve – arrange lamb on a large platter. Cut apricots into quarters and cut grapes into 8 little bunches. Arrange apricots and grapes around the edge of the platter and decorate with remaining mint leaves.

Cook's tip: I usually cook the lamb the day before I need it to give enough time for it to cool. When I buy the lamb, I get it boned as it is so much easier to carve. Allow 45 minutes per kilo plus an extra 20 minutes (20 minutes per lb plus extra 20 minutes).

1 roast leg lamb – cold See cook's tip below
1–2 handfuls fresh chopped coriander
2 handfuls fresh mint – chop half and keep half for decoration
4 heaped tsp mint jelly
500g (1lb) Greek yoghurt
4 fresh apricots
bunch of black seedless grapes – approx 450g(1lb)
salt and pepper

WATERCRESS, ROCKET AND BABY TOMATO SALAD

Rocket is an old fashioned salad herb which has always been popular in Italy and France but has recently been revived in Britain. It has a distinctive peppery taste and goes well with the watercress and sweetness of the cherry tomatoes.

Cut cherry tomatoes in half and pull the thick stalks off the watercress. Mix tomatoes and all leaves together in a large salad bowl. Toss in dressing before serving.

Cook's tip: You can now buy watercress in packets already washed.

250g (9oz) cherry tomatoes
2 bunches watercress (approx 75g each)
90g (3oz) rocket leaves
200g bag mixed salad leaves
8 tbsp ready-made French dressing

COUSCOUS WITH PINE NUTS·AND MARINATED VEGETABLES

350g (12oz) couscous
600ml (1pt) water
100g (3½oz) pine nuts
1 jar "Condiverde" – marinated Mediterranean vegetables (or marinated vegetables in oil, e.g. peppers, mushrooms, artichokes)
2 handfuls chopped parsley
juice of ½ lemon
3 tbsp olive oil
salt and pepper

Couscous is made from ground wheat. It is the same as semolina but has been rolled, dampened and coated with finer wheat flour. The beauty of couscous it that it can be used in salads without having to cook, all you need to do is soak it in water for about 20 minutes.

Leave couscous to soak in water for about 20 minutes or until the couscous has absorbed all the water. Mix in all remaining ingredients.

✻ May be made earlier in the day.

Serve at room temperature.

This recipe can also be served hot. Cover bowl with cling-film, leaving a gap for steam to escape, and microwave on high for 10 minutes.

Cook's tip: Make sure you add just the right amount of water to the couscous as it will soak up completely and save you having to drain it.

BLUEBERRY FILO TARTS

1 packet fresh filo pastry – or 8 sheets (measuring approx 30cm x 18cm)
2 tbsp olive oil
4 heaped tbsp icing sugar
400ml crème fraîche or fromage frais
250g (9oz) blueberries
Oven: 180°C, 350°F, Gas Mark 4

These tarts look very pretty. I prefer to use blueberries but other fruit may also be used, e.g. raspberries, blackberries, blackcurrants or other little berries. If these are out of season, frozen raspberries may be used, de-frosted and well drained.

Lay one sheet of filo out and lightly brush half of it with oil and fold in ½ to form a square. Brush ½ of this square with oil and fold in ½ again. Cut filo in ½ to form 2 squares (each will have 4 layers of filo). Put in tart tins and brush top of tarts with oil. Repeat this process until you have 16 tarts. Sprinkle with 1 tbsp of the icing sugar and cook in oven for 15 minutes until golden. Leave to cool.

◗ ✻ May be made up to this point 2 days before and stored in an air-tight container or may be frozen.

Mix crème fraîche or fromage frais with 2 heaped tbsp icing sugar and spoon into tarts. Put blueberries on top and sieve remaining icing sugar over the top.

ORDER OF PREPARATION IF MAKING IN ADVANCE:

The day before:
1. Cook lamb ☆
2. Marinate olives and feta.
3. Make croustades and egg mousse up to ◗
4. Make filo tarts to ◗

Earlier in the day:
5. Make lamb salad up to ◗
6. Make couscous.

In the evening:
7. Make watercress, rocket and tomato salad but do not dress until just before serving.
8. Finish off blueberry tarts.
9. Decorate lamb salad.
10. Finish off croustades with egg mousse

ORDER OF PREPARATION IN 2 HOURS (Cook lamb in advance a̶n̶d̶ ̶_____)
1. Marinate olive and feta.
2. Prepare egg croust_____
3. Make lamb salad.
4. Make filo t_rt_ _p _ ◗
5. Make cou___ __ ___
6. Make wa___ _____ tomato sala_
7. Finish off __lo ___
8. Finish off egg c____

BIGHT OF BANGKOCK

This menu was inspired by the type of food eaten around the coastal areas of Bangkok, known as the Bight of Bangkok. In this region food can be bought from floating markets. You are even able to jump from boat to boat to try out different dishes. Water is not a prerequisite for the following recipes, although it might make waves with your guests!

♀ A spicy white. Recommendation – Tokay, Pinot Gris, Mann – Alsace from France

TOMATO AND GOAT'S CHEESE PUFFS
ORIENTAL SEAFOOD SALAD
THAI RICE WITH LEMON GRASS AND LIME
PAWPAW AND LYCHEES SALAD
SUMMER FRUIT TERRINE

TOMATO AND GOAT'S CHEESE PUFFS

375g packet ready-rolled puff pastry
2 tbsp tomato purée
8 tomatoes
100g (3½oz) goat's cheese – sliced
Oven: 220ºC, 425ºF, Gas Mark 7

These light puff pastry squares are ideal to serve for your guests to eat in their fingers with drinks. Buy smallish tomatoes (not cherry) as slices of tomato will need to fit on to small squares.

Unroll pastry and cut into 32 squares (cutting 8 pieces across and 4 pieces down). Put on a baking tray and spread the tomato purée on top. Thinly slice the tomatoes and place a slice on each square, followed by the goat's cheese on top.

☀ May be prepared up to this point earlier in the day.

Put in oven for 20 minutes until golden and puffed up and serve immediately.

Cook's tip: Any type of goat's cheese may be used, firm or soft, and there is no need to remove the outer skin.

ORIENTAL SEAFOOD SALAD

350g (12oz) salmon fillets –
skinned

350g (12oz) haddock or cod –
skinned

350g (12oz) prawns – fresh or
frozen (de-frost if frozen)

8 spring onions – sliced

1 red chilli – de-seeded and
chopped or a few drops of
chilli sauce

3cm (1½") cube fresh root
ginger – chopped

1 tin (400ml) coconut milk

300g (11oz) yoghurt

1 bottle (150g) Stir-fry Teriyaki
Sauce – "Sharwoods"
recommended

1 tin (227g) water chestnuts –
drained and sliced

2 red peppers – de-seeded and
roughly chopped

2 handfuls chopped coriander

2 limes

salt and pepper

The chilli and ginger make this dish slightly spicy. The amounts can be increased if you prefer a really hot taste.

Remove any bones from salmon and haddock or cod and either put in microwave on high for approximately 5 minutes or poach in a frying pan with a little water for about 10 minutes or until cooked. Allow to cool and mix with all other ingredients except one red pepper, half the coriander and the limes.

❊ May be prepared up to this point earlier in the day.

To serve – put on a large platter, sprinkle remaining chopped red pepper and coriander on top, cut lime into wedges and arrange around the edge. Serve with Thai rice salad.

Cook's tip: To save time, ask the supermarket or fish monger to skin the fish for you.

THAI RICE WITH LEMON GRASS AND LIME

400g (14oz) Thai Jasmine rice

150g (5oz) French beans –
topped, tailed and sliced

150g (5oz) baby corn – sliced

1 handful chopped coriander

2 stalks of lemon grass – finely
chopped or 2 tsp ready-prepared
lemon grass

4 tbsp sesame oil

juice and zest of 1 lime

salt and pepper

Lemon grass is a commonly used ingredient in many Thai dishes. Don't be put off by its appearance, as it looks a bit like tough grass, but it has a lovely, distinctive citrus flavour. It is now available from most large supermarkets and oriental shops. Alternatively, it can be bought ready prepared, preserved in oil in small jars.

Put rice and beans in a large saucepan and cook according to instructions on the rice packet. Drain if necessary and mix with remaining ingredients. Allow to cool and serve cold.

❊ May be prepared earlier in the day.

Cook's tip: If you are not able to buy lemon grass, use the zest of 1 lemon instead.

*Opposite: The Ascot Picnic
(page 52)*

PAWPAW AND LYCHEES SALAD

1 ripe pawpaw or papaya

1 tin (approx 425g) lychees

1 iceberg or other crisp lettuce
–coarsely shredded

1 handful chopped mint

8 tbsp ready-made French
dressing

Pawpaw are abundant in Thailand and together with the lychees,
make this salad wonderfully refreshing.

Peel, de-seed and cut the pawpaw into chunks. Drain the lychees and cut in
half. Put the lettuce into a large salad bowl, add pawpaw, lychees and chopped
mint. Toss in dressing before serving.

*Cook's tip: The way of telling if a pawpaw is ripe is when the skin turns from
green to yellow. The pips of the pawpaw are edible but are very peppery – you
will either love them or hate them. As most people hate them, it's advisable not
to add them to the salad!*

SUMMER FRUIT TERRINE

1kg (2lbs 4oz) frozen mixed
summer fruit – do not de-frost

2 x 142g packets raspberry
flavour jelly

275ml (½pt) dry white wine

275ml (½pt) boiling water

This dessert is not necessarily typical of Thailand but, apart from fresh
fruit, not much is.

Line a terrine or loaf tin (1½ litres in capacity) with cling-film. Fill with frozen
summer fruit– if it won't all fit in, reserve some for decorating the terrine later.
Pull the jelly into cubes and dissolve in the boiling water (if necessary put in
microwave for about 1 minute to dissolve) and add white wine. Pour jelly
mixture over fruit and leave to set at room temperature for one hour. Put in
fridge until needed.

◗ May be made the day before.

To serve – turn terrine out onto a plate and remove cling-film. Put any
remaining fruit around the edge of the terrine and serve with cream, yoghurt or
fromage frais.

Cook's tip: Leaving the fruit frozen means that the jelly sets very quickly.

ORDER OF PREPARATION IF
MAKING IN ADVANCE:

The day before:
1. Make summer fruit terrine.

Earlier on the day:
2. Prepare tomato puffs up to ☀
3. Prepare oriental seafood up to ☀
4. Make Thai rice.

In the evening:
5. Prepare salad and toss in dressing
   before serving.
6. Decorate seafood.
7. Put tomato puffs in oven.

ORDER OF PREPARATION IN
UNDER 2 HOURS:

1. Make summer fruit terrine.
2. Make oriental seafood.
3. Make Thai rice and leave to cool.
4. Prepare tomato puffs and put in oven
   as necessary.
5. Prepare salad and toss in dressing
   before serving.

*Opposite: Rowing Up The Po
(page 37)*

A SUMMER BARBECUE

When you invite people round for a barbecue, they usually think of burnt sausages and under-cooked chicken! The recipes which follow will show you that barbecues can be a sumptuous feast.

For years I resisted buying a gas fired barbecue, feeling that part of the fun of barbecuing was all the preparation work. First rushing out to buy some charcoal, which I then normally smeared over my new white jeans. The next stage was trying to light the barbecue, then having to wait at least an hour before it was hot enough to use. This doesn't need to happen though if you are organised and make sure you buy plenty of charcoal and fire lighters. You should allow an hour between lighting it and starting to cook.

On the other hand, I now love my gas barbecue. You only have to light it 10 minutes before cooking. You can then control the temperature and it gives the food exactly the same barbecued flavour. If you are thinking about buying a new barbecue, I think it is well worth while spending a bit more and buying a gas one – I can assure you, you won't regret it.

BRUSCHETTA WITH FETA AND SUN-DRIED TOMATOES
MARINATED BUTTERFLY OF LAMB
VEGETABLE KEBABS
BABY BAKED POTATOES WITH CHEESY FROMAGE FRAIS AND CHIVES
BARBECUED BANANAS WITH RUM AND MASCARPONE

*♀ New World red.
Recommendation – Peter Lehmann, Vine Vale, Shiraz from Australia*

BRUSCHETTA WITH FETA AND SUN-DRIED TOMATOES

175g (6oz) feta cheese

1 jar (285g) sun-dried tomatoes in oil

1 loaf ciabatta bread

Oven: 200ºC, 400ºF, Gas Mark 6

Bruschetta is the Italian name for rustic, crusty bread, brushed with oil and toasted over coals. These days it is often toasted under a hot grill. This is an ideal starter for a barbecue as it can be passed round, eaten with pre-dinner drinks, allowing the "barbecuer" to toss and turn at the same time!

Put feta in a food processor with approximately ¾ of the sun-dried tomatoes and include some of the oil to form a paste.

Cut ciabatta into 16 slices and either put under a hot grill or on the barbecue to lightly toast. Brush one side with the remaining oil from the sun-dried tomatoes and spread the feta and tomato mixture on top. Slice the remaining sun-dried tomatoes and place these on the very top.

❉ May be prepared up to this point earlier in the day.

Put in oven for 10 minutes and serve hot.

Cook's tips: It is always handy to keep a loaf of ciabatta in the freezer. If people drop in unexpectedly you can always toast it, brush with oil, rub in garlic, and top with whatever you have in the fridge, e.g. any kind of cheese, pesto and chopped tomatoes, grilled red pepper and anchovies, the possibilities are limitless...

MARINATED BUTTERFLY OF LAMB

1 whole leg lamb – ask your butcher or supermarket to butterfly it, i.e. take out the bone, leaving two flaps

MARINADE

juice of 1 lemon

3 tbsp olive oil

3 garlic cloves – chopped

2 tsp mustard

1 tbsp soy sauce

2 handfuls chopped fresh rosemary

salt and pepper

Oven: 200ºC, 400ºF, Gas Mark 6

This is delicious cooked on a barbecue and nearly as good cooked in the oven. I am using a combination, a fool-proof method, which will ensure that the lamb is cooked perfectly. Lamb cooked in this way also makes an ideal Sunday lunch.

Mix all marinade ingredients together and marinate lamb for 1 hour or as long as possible.

◗ May be prepared the day before.

Cook lamb in oven for 25-30 minutes and then transfer to the barbecue for 25-30 minutes, basting regularly with marinade. Slice thickly and serve any remaining marinade.

Cook's tips: The timing of this will depend on whether you like your lamb pink in the middle or slightly better cooked. If you have a gas barbecue, always keep a spare cannister of gas in case one runs out at a crucial moment.

VEGETABLE KEBABS

300g (11oz) chestnut or button mushrooms

6 large courgettes

3 corn on the cob

olive oil

1 garlic clove – crushed

salt and pepper

8 kebab sticks – preferably metal

These kebabs are easy to cook and look great. If you can't be bothered to light the barbecue, they can also be done under a grill.

Wipe mushrooms and trim stalks if necessary. Wash courgettes and slice thickly. Slice corn into approximately 24 pieces in total. Thread vegetables onto kebab sticks. Drizzle oil over with crushed garlic and season.

☀ May be prepared up to this point earlier in the day.

Cook on barbecue for 20 minutes, turning frequently and brushing with oil and garlic.

Cook's tip: The corn on the cob can be quite tough to cut through and thread onto kebab sticks. So make sure you have a really sharp knife.

BABY BAKED POTATOES
WITH CHEESY FROMAGE FRAIS
AND CHIVES

1.5kg (3lbs 5oz) new potatoes

2 cartons (170g each) cheese and chive dip (sold in most supermarkets)

bunch chives – chopped

salt

Oven: 2   ºC, 400ºF, Gas Mark 6

Not many people think of baking new potatoes but they are delicious and always popular. On the rare occasions that you have any left over, they are also delicious eaten cold.

Scrub potatoes and rub salt into the skins while damp. Bake in oven for 1½ hours, turning half way through. They should be crunchy outside and soft inside.

Mix the cartons of dip with chopped chives and serve with potatoes.

Cook's tip: If you can't find the cheese and chive dip, use fromage frais and grated Parmesan.

BARBECUED BANANAS WITH RUM AND MASCARPONE

8 bananas

250g (9oz) Mascarpone

250g (9oz) Greek yoghurt

4 tbsp icing sugar

rum

Incredibly simple but wonderfully alcoholic and yummy.

Cut a slit horizontally in the banana skin, leaving the ends intact.

Pour approximately half a capful of rum into each banana and carefully wrap in foil to seal and stop any rum escaping.

Mix Mascarpone, Greek yoghurt, icing sugar and a slug of rum (3 tbsp or more) together. Serve in 8 ramekin dishes or one large bowl.

☀ May be prepared up to this point earlier in the day.

Cook bananas on barbecue for 10-15 minutes. Serve in foil with Mascarpone mixture.

Cook's tip: Buy some pineapple juice and coconut milk so that you can make yourself a pina colada while preparing this!

ORDER OF PREPARATION IF
MAKING IN ADVANCE:

The day before:
1. Marinate lamb.

Earlier on the day:
2. Prepare bruschetta up to ☀
3. Prepare vegetable kebabs up to ☀
4. Prepare bananas and dip up to ☀

In the evening:
5. Prepare potatoes and put in oven.
6. If using a charcoal barbecue, light one hour before you want to start cooking. For a gas barbecue, light 10 minutes before cooking.

7. Put lamb in oven and on barbecue as needed.
8. Put vegetable kebabs on barbecue as needed.
9. Put bruschetta in oven.
10. Barbecue bananas when needed.

ORDER OF PREPARATION IN 2 HOURS:
1. Marinate lamb for as long as possible and cook as needed.
2. Prepare and cook potatoes.
3. Light barbecue as in 6.
4. Prepare kebabs and barbecue when necessary.
5. Prepare bananas and barbecue when needed.
6. Make bruschetta.

SEAFOOD BARBECUE

Barbecues are great fun and a real social event. Gone are the days of images of camp fires with burnt sausages and a billy can of baked beans. Barbecues can now be a sophisticated event with sumptuous dishes. Fish tastes wonderful cooked on a barbecue and cooks in a very short time. A dense, firm fish is always the best for barbecuing and can be combined with shellfish.

If you are using a charcoal barbecue, light it one hour before you need to start cooking. For gas barbecues, light 10 minutes before cooking and always make sure you have a spare gas cannister in case you run out.

A lightly oaked Chardonnay and/or a soft light red (may be served chilled).
Recommendation –
Fetzer Sundial Chardonnay from California or Cono Sur, Pinot Noir (chilled) from Chile

MINI CRISPY TARTS OF MUSHROOMS, BACON AND BRIE
MARINATED PRAWN AND SWORDFISH KEBABS WITH LIME, CORIANDER AND GINGER
AVOCADO AND TOMATO SALSA
CHAR-GRILLED AUBERGINE, ROCKET AND PASTA SALAD
BARBECUED STUFFED NECTARINES WITH ALCOHOLIC FLAPJACKS

MINI CRISPY TARTS OF MUSHROOMS, BACON AND BRIE

Your guests can eat these mini crispy tarts in their fingers with drinks while the barbecuing takes place.

12 slices brown bread (thin or medium sliced)
olive oil
150g (5oz) button mushrooms – chopped
50g (2oz) bacon flavour soya bits
175g (6oz) brie
Oven: 190°C, 375°F, Gas Mark 5

Roll slices of bread with a rolling pin to flatten. With a round pastry cutter (approximately 6cm / 2½" in diameter) cut two rounds out of each slice of bread. Push the 24 rounds into tart tins and lightly brush with olive oil. Put in oven for 15 minutes until golden.

◗ May be made up to 2 days before and kept in an air-tight container.

Fill tarts with chopped mushrooms and soya bacon bits. Thinly slice brie, including the outside rind, and place a slice on top of each tart.

☀ May be prepared up to this point earlier in the day.

Put back in oven for 10-15 minutes until cheese has melted and serve.

Cook's tip: The bacon flavour soya bits are available from most supermarkets and really do taste of bacon. If you can't get hold of them, you can either use chopped ham or real bacon. If you use bacon, you will need to fry it first.

MARINATED PRAWN AND SWORDFISH KEBABS WITH LIME, CORIANDER AND GINGER

1kg (2lbs 4oz) swordfish steaks

32 tiger prawn tails – approx 400g (14oz) – preferably uncooked with shells on

1– 2 handfuls fresh coriander

2 garlic cloves

3cm (1¼") cube of fresh root ginger

4 tbsp olive oil

3 limes

salt and pepper

8 kebab sticks – metal or wooden

Swordfish and prawns are ideal for barbecuing. I prefer to use unshelled, uncooked prawns because they stay moister and taste fresher. I think it's good fun to let your guests peel their own prawns and, if you're eating outside, they can always wash their hands under the hose afterwards! If you think this is a real pain, then shelled prawns may be used instead.

Remove skin from swordfish and cut into 32 chunks. Thread onto kebab sticks alternating with prawns.

Put coriander with stalks, garlic, ginger, olive oil, 1 whole lime cut into quarters (skin pips and everything), salt and pepper into a food processor. If there are some tough pieces of lime rind which will not break up, then just remove them. Pour marinade over kebabs and leave to marinate for at least 1 hour.

◖ May be prepared up to this point the day before.

Put on a barbecue or under a hot grill for approximately 7 minutes turning half way through and basting with marinade. Cut remaining 2 limes into wedges and serve with kebabs.

Cook's tips: Brush the barbecue grill with oil before cooking as this will stop the fish sticking to it. If you are using wooden kebab sticks, soak them in water first to stop them burning.

AVOCADO AND TOMATO SALSA

1 red onion

1 garlic clove

2 ripe avocados

8 tomatoes – roughly chopped

4 tbsp mayonnaise

juice of ½ lemon

salt and pepper

This is a chunky salsa to serve with the kebabs.

Finely chop onion and garlic (may be done in a food processor). Peel and stone avocados and roughly mash with a fork. Mix together with chopped onion, garlic, tomatoes, mayonnaise, lemon juice, salt and pepper.

☀ May be prepared earlier in the day.

Cook's tip: Put the onion and garlic in the food processor directly after processing the marinade for the kebabs. A small amount of left over marinade will only add to the salsa and save washing up.

CHAR-GRILLED AUBERGINE, ROCKET AND PASTA SALAD

2 large aubergine

8 tbsp olive oil

500g (1lb 2oz) fresh or dried pasta – shells or bows

60g (2½oz) rocket

1 green pepper – de-seeded and chopped

1 tub (170g) hummus

1 tbsp balsamic vinegar

salt and pepper

French dressing may be used instead of hummus in this salad.

Slice the aubergines into rounds, brush both sides with 4 tbsp of the oil and season. Either put under a very hot grill or on a barbecue for approximately 10 minutes until well charred on both sides. Cut rounds in half. Cook pasta according to instructions on packet and drain. Mix pasta with aubergine and leave to cool. (Aubergine may be cooked later on the barbecue and added to the salad while hot.)

☼ May be prepared up to this point earlier in the day.

Put pasta and aubergine into a large salad bowl, add all remaining ingredients, toss and serve.

BARBECUED STUFFED NECTARINES WITH ALCOHOLIC FLAPJACKS

8 large nectarines

250g (9oz) raspberries – fresh or frozen

250g (9oz) Mascarpone

2 tbsp icing sugar

8 ready-made flapjacks

large slug of sweet alcohol (8 tsp) – anything you have handy or want to get rid of, e.g. sweet sherry, port, Cointreau

The nectarines are wrapped in foil and put on the barbecue.

Cut nectarines in half and remove the stone. Stuff about 4 raspberries into one side of the cavity and a teaspoon of Mascarpone into the other. Sandwich together and wrap tightly in foil. Mix remaining raspberries and Mascarpone together with the sugar.

☼ May be prepared up to this point earlier in the day.

Cut flapjacks in half horizontally, spread Mascarpone mixture on the bottom half and put the other half back on top. Pour 1 teaspoon of liqueur over each flapjack and leave to soak in. Put nectarines on to the outside or cooler part of the barbecue for 10 minutes or alternatively in the oven: 180°C, 350°F, Gas Mark 4 for 10 minutes. Serve wrapped in the foil for your guests to unwrap with the alcoholic flapjacks.

ORDER OF PREPARATION IF MAKING IN ADVANCE:

The day before:
1. Make mini tarts up to ◑
2. Marinate fish kebabs.

Earlier on the day:
3. Fill mini tarts up to ☼
4. Make avocado and tomato salsa.
5. Grill or barbecue aubergine and make pasta salad but do not add rocket until just before serving.
6. Prepare nectarines up to ☼

In the evening:
7. If using a charcoal barbecue, light one hour before you need to start cooking. For a gas barbecue, light 10 minutes before cooking.
8. Heat mini tarts.
9. Barbecue fish kebabs.
10. Make alcoholic flapjacks and barbecue nectarines when needed.

ORDER OF PREPARATION IN UNDER 2 HOURS:
1. Marinate fish kebabs and barbecue when needed.
2. Make avocado and tomato salsa.
3. Light barbecue as in 7 above.
4. Make mini tarts.
5. Prepare pasta salad. Char-grill aubergine as needed and toss into salad with rocket before serving.
6. Prepare stuffed nectarines and flapjacks and barbecue nectarines when needed.

BLOWING HOT AND COLD

This is a very versatile menu as it can be served hot or cold for a dinner party or buffet.

HOT CARAMELISED BACON, SPINACH AND CROUTON SALAD
SERVED WITH GARLIC AND SUN-DRIED TOMATO BREAD
FILLET OF BEEF WITH BÉARNAISE SAUCE
ROAST VEGETABLE PLATTER
OREGANO NEW POTATOES
FRENCH RASPBERRY TART

New World Cabernet Sauvignon. Recommendation – Seaview, Cabernet Sauvignon from Australia

HOT CARAMELISED BACON, SPINACH AND CROUTON SALAD

400g baby spinach leaves (can be bought in bags ready-washed)

4 tbsp olive oil

2 tbsp honey

225g (8oz) rindless bacon – chopped

1 tbsp balsamic vinegar

100g packet croutons

My friend Rebecca came back from a skiing holiday raving about a wonderful salad she had eaten in a French restaurant. Together we recreated it and this is what we came up with – very simple but very yummy.

Put spinach in a large salad bowl. Heat 1 tbsp of the oil and 1 tbsp honey in a frying pan until frothing. Add bacon and fry until golden. Take bacon out of frying pan with a slotted spoon and keep warm. Add remaining oil and honey to pan with 1 tbsp balsamic vinegar and mix together over a gentle heat. Add bacon and croutons to spinach, pour dressing from the pan, toss and serve with warm bread – see Handy Hints page 5.

Cook's tip: The hot bacon and dressing make this salad so unusual. If you don't want to cook the bacon at the last minute, it can be made in advance and left to cool with the dressing. If you're feeling really lazy you can use "bacon flavour soya chips" (pretend bacon) which doesn't need cooking.

GARLIC AND SUN-DRIED TOMATO BREAD

1 loaf ciabatta

100g (3½oz) crushed sun-dried tomatoes

1 garlic clove – crushed

Oven: 190ºC, 375ºF, Gas Mark 5

A pleasant change from the usual boring garlic bread.

Cut ciabatta in half lengthways. Mix sun-dried tomatoes with garlic and spread on each side of the ciabatta. Sandwich together and wrap in foil.

✻ May be prepared up to this point earlier in the day.

Put in oven for 15 minutes, slice and serve.

Cook's tip: You can use this method of cutting the bread lengthways when making any type of garlic bread. It takes a fraction of the time. You'll probably spit for not thinking of it yourself.

FILLET OF BEEF WITH BÉARNAISE SAUCE

1.5kg (3lbs 5oz) beef fillet
2 tbsp olive oil
pepper
1 jar (250ml) Béarnaise Sauce
1 bunch watercress
Oven: 230ºC, 450ºF, Gas Mark 8

Cooking beef for a dinner party can be a nightmare if your guests arrive late and the beef is burnt. In this recipe, the beef is cooked in a very hot oven for a short time so you don't have to start cooking it until all your guests have arrived. Fillet beef is expensive but you can be sure that it will be deliciously tender. The jars of Béarnaise sauce that you can now buy at supermarkets and delis are really good and no one would know that you didn't make it yourself (unless you leave the jar lying around). I served this at my Mother's 70th birthday party and even her vegetarian friend ate it – the first time she'd eaten meat in 10 years!

Trim any excess fat off the fillet. Rub with oil and season with pepper. Leave to stand for 1-2 hours at room temperature before cooking.

❋ May be prepared up to this point earlier in the day.

Put in a roasting tin and cook for 25 minutes per kilo (12 minutes per lb). Either carve into thick slices and serve immediately decorated with watercress or leave to cool and eat cold.

Béarnaise sauce – either put in microwave on low for 2 minutes or stand jar in a bowl of very hot water for 5 minutes. Heat the sauce gradually otherwise it may curdle.

N.B. If beef is being served cold, do not heat the Béarnaise sauce – serve cold as well.

Cook's tip: Don't put the beef in the oven too early. You will only worry that it will be over cooked and you will force your guests to eat their starter faster than the speed of sound! Put it in the oven just before you sit down to eat your starter. It is better to have a relaxed starter and linger in the knowledge that your beef will be perfect. Stick religiously to the cooking times above and I can assure you it will be perfect – trust me.

ROAST VEGETABLE PLATTER

2 aubergines – thickly sliced into rounds
6 courgettes – cut in half lengthways and then cut across horizontally
4 medium onions – peeled and cut into quarters
2 red and 2 yellow peppers – de- eeded and cut into 6
'ic cloves – crushed
' tbsp o   'l
'alsa   ar
anc
Ov   ., 42   lark

A popular and effective way to cook vegetables which need little last minute attention. Some recipes tell you to sprinkle salt over the sliced aubergines and leave them for 30 minutes. I think this is a complete waste of time as it doesn't make the slightest bit of difference. It is the seeds in the aubergine that can sometimes make them bitter and, apparently, the male aubergine have fewer seeds than the female. So when you go shopping, ask specially for male aubergines.

Group vegetables together in a large roasting tin or two with garlic scattered over them. Pour olive oil on top and season. Roast in oven for 1 hour, tossing occasionally but keeping same vegetables grouped together.
Arrange on a platter, pour over balsamic vinegar.

May be served hot or cold.

Cook's tip: If you have any vegetables left over, buy a French loaf and put them inside. They make a delicious sandwich to eat the next day.

OREGANO NEW POTATOES

1½ kg (3lbs) new potatoes

250g (8oz) fromage frais

1 handful fresh chopped oregano

salt and pepper

Oregano and marjoram belong to the same family and have similar properties. Fresh herbs give a much better flavour to these potatoes, so if you can't find oregano, use marjoram instead.

Put new potatoes into boiling water and simmer for 15 minutes. Mix other ingredients together. Drain potatoes and toss in fromage frais mixture. If serving cold, allow potatoes to cool, then toss in fromage frais mixture.

Cook's tip: Take the potatoes off the heat before you toss in fromage frais otherwise it will curdle.

FRENCH RASPBERRY TART

250g (9oz) short crust pastry – can be bought fresh or frozen

300g (11oz) raspberries

300ml (½pt) crème fraîche

4 heaped tbsp brown sugar

3 eggs

Oven: 190°C, 375°F, Gas Mark 5

A lovely fresh summer tart. Other fruit may be used instead or as well as raspberries, e.g. blueberries, blackberries, stoned cherries.

Roll out pastry and line a tart tin or flan dish (preferably loose-bottomed) 25cm-26cm in diameter. Prick base with a fork and bake in oven for 10 minutes. If bubbles appear just push them down with the back of a spoon. Put raspberries into pastry case. Beat or whisk together eggs, crème fraîche and 3 tbsp of the brown sugar. Pour over raspberries and sprinkle remaining 1 tbsp brown sugar on top. Cook for 25 minutes.

◗ ❄ May be made the day before or may be frozen.

May be served hot or cold.

To re-heat – put in oven for 15 minutes.

Cook's tip: If you are using a loose-bottomed tart tin, remove sides but leave tart on the base – it could be disastrous if you tried to take it off! If you are in a real hurry, you can use ready-made tart pastry cases. As they look a bit "bought" you will have to bash them around to give them the home-made look.

ORDER OF PREPARATION IF MAKING IN ADVANCE:

The day before:
1. Make raspberry tart.

Earlier on the day:
2. Make garlic and sun-dried tomato bread.
3. Prepare the beef up to ❄

In the evening:
4. Prepare the vegetables and cook as necessary.
5. Prepare potatoes and cook as necessary.
6. Calculate cooking time for beef and put in oven at correct time, warm Béarnaise.
7. Make starter.
8. Re-heat raspberry tart while eating main course.

If you are going to serve the main course cold, the beef and roast vegetables can be cooked the day before and the potatoes can be cooked earlier on the day.

ORDER OF PREPARATION IN 2 HOURS:
1. Prepare beef and put in oven at calculated time. Heat Béarnaise when needed.
2. Prepare tart and cook during main course.
3. Prepare roast vegetables and put in oven as needed.
4. Prepare potatoes and fromage frais mixture and cook as needed.
5. Make garlic and sun-dried tomato bread.
6. Make salad.

CANARIAN EXPERIENCE

I have spent many holidays in Tenerife and travelled around some of the other islands in the Canaries. It is rejuvenating to go during the winter to escape the cold and bask in warm temperatures. Unfortunately, many of the restaurants serve "English Fish and Chips", "Roast Beef and Yorkshire Pudding" which are very pleasant to eat while in England but the type of food I try to avoid whilst on holiday. After years of practise I have sought out some wonderful typically Canarian restaurants and it is from these that I have gained inspiration for the following recipes.

CHEATS GAZPACHO
BAKED COD WITH SALSA VERDE
CANARIAN POTATO, RED PEPPER AND ONION BAKE
TOMATO, CANNELLINI BEAN AND ASPARAGUS SALAD
FRESH PINEAPPLE WITH PASSION FRUIT AND ELDERFLOWER ICE CREAM

A ripe fruity white. Recommendation – Vega Sindoa Barrel Fermented Chardonnay, Navarra from Spain

CHEATS GAZPACHO

A lovely light soup, full of different flavours, to serve on a warm summer evening.

1 large tin (435g) "Heinz Tomato Soup"
1.5 litres (2½pts) tomato juice
2 garlic cloves – crushed
½ cucumber – chopped
2 tbsp balsamic vinegar
salt and pepper
TO SERVE IN SEPARATE BOWLS
1 red pepper – de-seeded and chopped
1 yellow pepper – de-seeded and chopped
8 spring onions – chopped
1 packet small croutons

Mix together all soup ingredients and chill.

◗ This is best left for a few hours or overnight for ingredients to infuse.

Prepare ingredients to serve separately and put into bowls for people to help themselves.

Serve with warm Spanish or French bread. See Handy Hints Page 5.

Cook's tips: Don't be put off by the "Heinz" soup. It actually adds a wonderful flavour without anyone realising where it came from. If you need to chill the soup quickly, add a few ice cubes.

BAKED COD WITH SALSA VERDE

2kg (4lbs 8oz) cod fillets – skinned
2 lemons – cut into 8 wedges
SALSA VERDE
4 handfuls fresh parsley (approx 70g)
1 small jar capers
3 garlic cloves
juice of 1 lemon
200ml (12tbsp) olive oil
3 tsp sugar
salt and pepper
Oven: 200ºC, 400ºF, Gas Mark 6

I have often eaten a fish called "Bacolao" cooked in this way and loved it. I had assumed it was a rather exotic fish only found in warm waters and was amazed when I discovered it was cod. Salsa means "sauce" in Spanish.

To make salsa verde – reserve a few sprigs of parsley for decoration and put remainder in a food processor with capers and garlic. Add remaining ingredients and blend. Put fish in an oven-proof serving dish in one layer and marinate in approximately a third of the salsa verde for at least one hour.

◗ May be prepared up to this point the day before.

Cover fish with foil and cook in oven for 25 minutes, removing the foil half way through cooking.

Serve fish with lemon wedges and reserved parsley. Put remaining salsa verde in a bowl for people to help themselves.

Cook's tip: The salsa verde will keep in the fridge for up to a week. It is also delicious with chicken, baked potatoes or tossed into salads.

CANARIAN POTATO, RED PEPPER AND ONION BAKE

2 onions – sliced
2 red peppers – de-seeded and sliced
8 medium-sized potatoes – scrubbed
4 tbsp olive oil
salt and pepper
Oven: 200ºC, 400ºF, Gas Mark 6

A delicious and unusual way of baking potatoes.

Grease a large oven-proof serving dish. Put sliced onions and peppers in the bottom. Cut potatoes in half horizontally, through the thinnest part and put in one layer on top of onions and peppers. Pour olive oil over and season generously.

Cook in oven for one hour.

Cook's tip: The potatoes may be served straight from the dish they are cooked in or, if you prefer, you can cook them in a roasting tin and transfer them to a serving dish once cooked.

TOMATO, CANNELLINI BEAN AND ARTICHOKE SALAD

4 large beef tomatoes – sliced

150g (5oz) cherry tomatoes – cut in half

1 tin (440g) cannellini beans – drained

1 tin (440g) artichoke hearts – drained and cut in half

8 tbsp ready-made French dressing

1 handful fresh chopped oregano or marjoram (optional)

salt and pepper

Tomatoes grow in abundance in the Canaries so they are very popular in salads. Choose ripe, juicy tomatoes that are full of flavour.

Arrange sliced beef tomatoes on a large platter or flat bowl. Scatter cherry tomatoes, cannellini beans and artichoke hearts on top. Season, pour dressing over salad and sprinkle with chopped herbs.

Cook's tip: Tinned asparagus could be used instead of artichokes for a change.

FRESH PINEAPPLE WITH PASSION FRUIT AND ELDERFLOWER ICE CREAM

1 litre good quality vanilla ice cream

8 passion fruit

4 tbsp elderflower cordial

1 pineapple

A deliciously refreshing dessert. Elderflower cordial is available from most supermarkets and is well worth buying as it makes a lovely drink when diluted with sparkling water.

Allow ice cream to soften slightly. Scoop out inside of passion fruit and mix with ice cream and elderflower cordial. Return to freezer for at least 2 hours.

❋ May be made up to this point and kept in freezer until needed.

Remove skin of pineapple, slice and core. Serve with ice cream.

Cook's tip: If you are really pushed for time, you can now buy fresh pineapple ready peeled and sliced.

ORDER OF PREPARATION IF MAKING IN ADVANCE:

The day before:
1. Make gazpacho up to ◖
2. Prepare cod and salsa verde up to ◖
3. Make ice cream.

In the evening:
4. Prepare ingredients to serve with gazpacho.
5. Make tomato, cannellini bean and artichoke salad.
6. Prepare and cook potatoes.
7. Peel and slice pineapple.
8. Cook cod when necessary.

ORDER OF PREPARATION IN UNDER 2 HOURS.
1. Make ice cream.
2. Make gazpacho.
3. Prepare cod and salsa verde and cook as needed.
4. Prepare and cook potatoes.
5. Make salad.
6. Slice pineapple.

CHILL OUT FOR SUMMER

The last thing you want to do on a hot summers day is spend it in an even hotter steamy kitchen. This menu is designed so that you can spend all day lazing round a pool, playing tennis or even gardening if you have to! It is full of lovely cool, fruity flavours and, as nothing has to be cooked at the last minute, is ideal to serve outside. Why not keep cool, move a table and chairs out into the garden and eat "al fresco"?

♀ New World Chardonnay. Recommendation – Peter Lehmann, Vine Vale Chardonnay from Australia

CHILLED CUCUMBER, YOGHURT AND MINT SOUP
CHICKEN BREASTS WITH MANGO AND POPPY SEEDS
IN A MANGO VINAIGRETTE
NUTTY WILD RICE SALAD
AVOCADO, GRAPEFRUIT AND CHICORY SALAD
HAZELNUT AND RASPBERRY ROULADE WITH A RASPBERRY COULIS

CHILLED CUCUMBER, YOGHURT AND MINT SOUP

2 cucumbers
500ml natural yoghurt
600ml (1pt) milk
2 handfuls fresh chopped mint
salt and pepper
freshly baked rolls – see Cook's tip below (optional)

A wonderfully cool, refreshing soup for a hot summers day.

Wash the cucumbers, cut ends off but leave skin on and grate (may be done in a food processor). Put grated cucumber and juice into a large bowl and mix together with yoghurt, milk, half the chopped mint, salt and pepper. Chill.

◗ May be made the day before.

Sprinkle remaining chopped mint on top and serve with rolls.

Cook's tip: Buy 2 packets "French Experience" mini baguettes (bread dough). Open packets, separate rolls and sprinkle poppy or sesame seeds on top. Baking as instructions on packet.

CHICKEN BREASTS WITH MANGO AND POPPY SEEDS IN A MANGO VINAIGRETTE

2 large ripe mangos

6 tbsp olive oil

2 tbsp balsamic vinegar

1 tsp curry powder

100g bag mixed salad leaves

8 ready-cooked chicken breasts – skinned

2 tbsp poppy seeds

salt and pepper

Oven: 190°C, 375°F, Gas Mark 5

This is a lovely light fruity recipe. The combination of the orange mango and black poppy seeds looks stunning on the plate.

Peel mangos, cut flesh from either side of the stone and cut into strips.

To make mango vinaigrette – cut off remaining mango round the stone and put in a food processor or liquidizer with olive oil, vinegar, curry powder, salt and pepper.

☼ May be prepared earlier in the day.

To serve – arrange salad leaves on each plate. Slice the chicken breasts and fan out on top of leaves. Pour vinaigrette over the chicken and sprinkle poppy seeds on top. Decorate with slices of mango.

Cook's tip: Mango does not discolour, so it's quite safe to cut it into strips in the morning and keep it in a fridge covered with cling-film.

NUTTY WILD RICE SALAD

400g (14oz) mixed long-grain and wild rice

100g (3½oz) roasted salted peanuts

100g (3½oz) sunflower seeds

8 spring onions – chopped

8 tbsp ready-made French dressing

salt and pepper

This lovely crunchy rice salad is made so easy now that you can buy packets of long-grain and wild rice ready mixed.

Cook rice according to instructions on packet and drain. Mix with all remaining ingredients and leave to cool.

☼ May be made earlier in the day.

Cook's tip: Other nuts or seeds may also be used, e.g. cashew, walnuts, pecans and pumpkin seeds.

AVOCADO, GRAPEFRUIT AND CHICORY SALAD

2 large ripe avocados

juice of ½ lemon

4-5 heads of chicory

1 tin (450g) grapefruit segments

DRESSING

6 tbsp olive oil

2 tbsp balsamic vinegar

½ tsp sugar

2 handfuls fresh mint – chop half and reserve half for decoration

salt and pepper

The slight bitterness of the chicory and grapefruit go exceptionally well with the sweetness of the mango chicken.

Peel and slice avocados and toss in lemon juice to stop discolouring. Slice chicory and drain grapefruit. Arrange on a large platter or salad bowl. Mix all dressing ingredients together (except mint leaves for decorations) and pour over the salad. Decorate with little sprigs of remaining mint.

◖ The dressing can be made a few days in advance.

Cook's tip: If you want to save time, use a ready-made dressing.

HAZELNUT AND RASPBERRY ROULADE WITH A RASPBERRY COULIS

5 eggs

175g (6oz) castor sugar

100g (3½oz) ground hazelnuts

300ml (½pt) double cream

125g (4oz) fresh raspberries

COULIS

250g (9oz) fresh or frozen raspberries – de-frosted

juice 1 lemon

slug cassis – approx 4 tbsp

2 tbsp icing sugar

Oven: 190°C, 375°F, Gas Mark 5

There isn't much cheating in this recipe, but it is so simple to make and people never fail to be impressed with roulades, especially when they are served with a coulis.

Grease a swiss roll tin and line with baking parchment. Separate the eggs and whisk the whites until stiff. Whisk yolks with sugar until light and fluffy. Fold in ground hazelnuts and egg whites. Put into prepared tin and cook for 15 minutes. Leave to cool. Put another piece of baking parchment on top and cover with a damp tea towel. Whisk cream until stiff.

To make coulis – put all coulis ingredients in a food processor or liquidizer to purée and pour into a jug.

❋ May be prepared up to this point the day before but the tea towel covering the roulade must be kept damp. May also be frozen.

Turn roulade out of tin on to the baking parchment. Spread cream over the roulade.

Reserve half the fresh raspberries and scatter the other half over the cream. Roll up the roulade, using the baking parchment to help and decorate with remaining raspberries.

Slice roulade and serve with coulis.

Cook's tip: If you whisk the egg white first, you don't have to wash the whisk before whisking the yolks. Don't panic if the roulade forms cracks when rolling up – just cover them with raspberries or raspberry coulis.

ORDER OF PREPARATION IF MAKING IN ADVANCE:

The day before:
1. Make cucumber soup.
2. Make roulade up to ❋
3. Make dressing for salad.

Earlier on the day:
4. Prepare mango vinaigrette.
5. Make rice salad.

In the evening:
6. Roll up roulade.
7. Make avocado salad.
8. Finish off chicken recipe.
9. Cook the bread dough.

ORDER OF PREPARATION IN UNDER 2 HOURS:
1. Make soup and chill.
2. Make roulade up to ❋
3. Make rice salad.
4. Make chicken and mango recipe.
5. Make avocado salad.
6. Roll up roulade.
7. Cook bread dough.

A GREEK ANALOGY

I once spent six months working on the small Greek island of Andros. Most of the food was shipped over from the mainland but on windy days, with rough seas, the ferry was cancelled and the shops were empty. Cooking was a nightmare as I was working in a minute kitchen with small fridge and ice box freezer. I became a genius at creating many different gourmet recipes out of tinned tuna. I can assure you that there is no tinned tuna in these recipes, however. I hope the tastes in this menu will inspire memories of sunny days and warm balmy evenings. If you feel so inclined, the meal can be finished off with a quick Zorba's dance followed by some plate smashing – expensive but saves on the washing up!

CHICK-PEA AND CAULIFLOWER À LA GRECQUE WITH OLIVE BREAD
MARINATED LAMB KEBABS WITH TZATZIKI ON A BED OF
MINTED BULGUR WHEAT WITH APRICOTS AND RAISINS
ROAST COURGETTES, PEPPERS AND TOMATOES WITH FETA
ALMOND TARTLETTES WITH HONEYED GREEK YOGHURT

*♀ A fruity, oaky red.
Recommendation – Palacio de la
Vega Crianza from Spain*

CHICK-PEA AND CAULIFLOWER À LA GRECQUE WITH OLIVE BREAD

Chick-peas are often used in Greek cooking but are best known used in hummus. They can be bought dried but need soaking overnight and this is why the tins of chick-peas are so handy as they are ready to eat. In this recipe they are marinated with cauliflower and served cold.

8 tbsp olive oil
2 glasses dry white wine
1 handful fresh chopped thyme
2 garlic cloves – crushed or chopped
2 onions – chopped
1 large or 2 small cauliflowers
1 large tin (800g) tomatoes
2 tins (440g each) chick-peas
salt and pepper
Greek olive bread

Put oil, wine, thyme, garlic, salt and pepper into a large saucepan and bring to the boil. Add chopped onions and allow to simmer gently for 5 minutes. Break cauliflower up into little florets and add to saucepan with tin of tomatoes with the juice. Simmer for a further 10 minutes. Drain chick-peas and add to saucepan. Leave to cool and marinate for at least 1½ hours before serving.

◗ May be prepared the day before.

Serve with warm olive bread – see Handy Hints page 5.

Cook's tip: Olive bread (bread with chunks or whole olives in it) can be bought from most large supermarkets, but if you have problems finding it, use ciabatta instead.

MARINATED LAMB KEBABS WITH TZATZIKI

Lamb kebabs, known as "souvlaki" and tzatziki are both typically Greek. It is not necessarily typical for them to be served together, as tzatziki is usually served as a starter, but the flavours go amazingly well together.

1 tub (300g-350g) tzatziki

2 tbsp olive oil

2 garlic cloves – crushed

2 lemons – squeeze 1 and cut the other into 8 wedges

1.2kg (2½ lbs) boned leg of lamb (or buy already diced leg of lamb suitable for kebabs)

4 red onions

salt and pepper

8 kebab sticks – metal or wooden

Oven: 200ºC, 400ºF, Gas Mark 6

To make the marinade – mix together half the tzatziki, the olive oil, garlic, juice of one lemon and season. Cut lamb into bite size pieces, if not already done. Peel and quarter onions and separate into layers. Thread lamb and onion onto 8 skewers, alternating pieces. Put in an oven-proof dish, pour marinade over lamb kebabs and leave to marinate for at least one hour.

◗ May be prepared up to this point the day before.

Cook in oven for 40 minutes, turning half way through. Serve on a bed of bulgur wheat with the juices from the pan and the remaining tzatziki spooned over kebabs. Put a wedge of lemon on each plate.

Cook's tip: The kebabs are also ideal to cook on a BBQ, using the marinade to baste them. If using wooden kebab sticks, soak them in water first to stop them burning.

MINTED BULGUR WHEAT WITH APRICOTS AND RAISINS

Bulgur wheat is also knows as cracked wheat. This is because it starts as a wheat grain which is boiled and cracks in the process. It makes a pleasant change from rice or potatoes and has a wonderfully light, nutty taste.

300g (11oz) bulgur wheat

150g (5oz) raisins or sultanas

150g (5oz) dried apricots – sliced

2 handfuls fresh mint – chopped but reserve a few leaves for decoration

salt and pepper

Put bulgur wheat in a saucepan with plenty of cold water. Bring to boil and simmer for 10 minutes. Drain well, return to the saucepan and add remaining ingredients except the mint for decoration.

❋ May be prepared up to this point earlier in the day and re-heated in a microwave on high for 7 minutes.

Serve with lamb kebabs on top and decorate with remaining mint leaves.

Cook's tip: It's very important to drain the bulgur wheat well otherwise it will become soggy.

ROAST COURGETTES, PEPPERS AND TOMATOES WITH FETA

200g (7oz) feta cheese– cut into cubes (approx 1cm / ½")

4 tbsp olive oil

juice of ½ lemon

8 courgettes – cut in half lengthways and then cut across horizontally

2 garlic cloves – thinly sliced

4 yellow peppers – de-seeded and cut in quarters

500g (1lb 2oz) cherry tomatoes

salt and pepper

Oven: 200ºC, 400ºF, Gas Mark 6

This is rather like a baked Greek salad but even better.

Mix cubes of feta with 1 tbsp of the olive oil and the lemon juice and leave to marinate until ready to cook. Put courgettes, garlic, remaining oil and salt and pepper in a large roasting dish and put in oven for 1 hour, tossing occasionally. After the first 30 minutes add peppers and tomatoes. Add feta with marinade 5 minutes before the end of the cooking time.

Cook's tip: This is also delicious served cold. To do this, cook the vegetables as above, leave to cool and then toss in feta with marinade.

ALMOND TARTLETTES WITH HONEYED GREEK YOGHURT

225g ready-made short crust pastry

apricot jam

75g (3oz) butter

3 level tbsp castor sugar

3 eggs

100g (3½oz) ground almonds

2 heaped tbsp self-raising flour

few drops almond essence

400g Greek yoghurt

3 tbsp runny honey

Oven: 180ºC, 350ºF, Gas Mark 4

These crisp little tarts are ideal for picnics too.

Roll out pastry thinly on a lightly floured work surface. Using a round pastry cutter (approximately 6cm / 2½" in diameter) cut out as many circles as you can – around 20-24. Put in tart tins, prick the bottom with a fork and put half a teaspoon of apricot jam in each.

Put butter and sugar in a food processor or mixer until smooth. Add eggs, ground almonds, flour, almond essence and 1 heaped tbsp apricot jam. Process or mix until smooth. Put mixture into prepared tartlette cases and put in oven for 20 minutes. Mix Greek yoghurt with honey and serve with warm tarts.

◖❄ The tarts may be made the day before or frozen.

To re-heat – put tarts back in oven for 10 minutes.

Cook's tip: The quantity above will be enough for 10-12 people but remember, if you have any left over, you can freeze them (assuming they haven't already been).

ORDER OF PREPARATION IF
MAKING IN ADVANCE:

The day before:
1. Make starter.
2. Marinate kebabs.
3. Make almond tartlettes and prepare yoghurt and honey.

Earlier on the day:
4. Make bulgar wheat recipe.

In the evening:
5. Marinate feta, prepare roast vegetables and put in oven as needed.
6. Put kebabs in oven as needed.

7. Re-heat bulgur wheat.
8. Warm Greek bread.
9. Re-heat tarts while eating main course.

ORDER OF PREPARATION IN
UNDER 2 HOURS:
1. Make starter and leave to cool.
2. Prepare kebabs and leave to marinate – cook when necessary.
3. Make almond tartlettes and prepare yoghurt. Re-heat during main course.
4. Marinate feta, prepare roast vegetables and put in oven as needed.
5. Make bulgur wheat.
6. Warm bread.

A "NO COOK" DINNER OR BUFFET PARTY

Did you ever think you could prepare a whole dinner or buffet without even having to turn on the oven? Well, it is possible and you will find these recipes ideal for hot summer days when the last thing you feel like doing is slaving over a hot oven.

GRAVADLAX AND PRAWNS ON PUMPERNICKEL WITH A DILL SAUCE
MANGO CHICKEN WITH CASHEW NUTS
TABBOULEH
MANGETOUT AND BABY TOMATOES IN A MUSTARD VINAIGRETTE
ICED LEMON TERRINE WITH A BOOZY BLUEBERRY COULIS

♀ *A ripe slightly spicy white.*
Recommendation –
Pinot Blanc, Mann – Alsace
from France

GRAVADLAX AND PRAWNS ON PUMPERNICKEL WITH A DILL SAUCE

An impressive starter with a Ferring (Scandinavian) feel. Gravadlax is marinated raw salmon and is often served with dill.

8 slices pumpernickel bread

150g (5oz) gravadlax

200g (7oz) prawns

1 handful fresh sprigs of dill

½ jar (approx. 80g) dill mustard or dill sauce

2 heaped tbsp fromage frais (approx. 125g)

100g bag mixed salad leaves

1 lemon – sliced

Cut slices of pumpernickel in half. Arrange gravadlax on 8 of the halves and divide prawns between the other 8. Chop half the dill and mix with dill sauce and fromage frais. Put a blob on top of the gravadlax and prawns and place a sprig of dill on top. Either arrange on individual serving plates, or on a big platter with salad leaves and lemon slices.

Cook's tip: These can be served with drinks for guests to eat in their fingers. If you are going to do this, you will need to cut the pumpernickel into quarters to make them easier to handle.

MANGO CHICKEN WITH CASHEW NUTS

1 large or 2 small mangos
5 heaped tbsp mayonnaise
200g (7oz) yoghurt
2 tsp curry powder
2 heaped tbsp mango chutney
2 ready-cooked chickens or 8 ready-cooked chicken breasts
100g (3½oz) roast cashew nuts (it does not matter whether they are salted or not)
2 heads chicory
salt and pepper

A welcome change from coronation chicken. The mango gives this dish a lovely fresh fruity taste. Buy ready-cooked chicken available from most supermarkets.

Peel mango, cut flesh off each side of the stone and cut into strips for decoration. Cut off remaining mango around the stone and blend in a food processor with mayonnaise, yoghurt, curry powder, mango chutney, salt and pepper.

Remove skin from chickens, pull flesh off the bone and cut into bite-size pieces.

◗ May be prepared up to this point the day before.

Mix mango mayonnaise with chicken and half the cashew nuts.

To serve – cut base off the chicory and separate leaves. Arrange them around the outside of a large serving platter or bowl. Put mango chicken in the middle and decorate with remaining cashew nuts and mango strips.

Cook's tip: Mango does not discolour so it is OK to prepare it in advance as long as you cover it with cling-film and keep in a fridge.

TABBOULEH

200g (7oz) bulgur wheat
8 spring onions – chopped
½ cucumber – chopped
1 yellow pepper – de-seeded and chopped
2 handfuls fresh chopped mint
2 handfuls fresh chopped parsley
4 tbsp olive oil
juice 1 lemon
salt and pepper

A quick, colourful salad, full of herbs, which originates from the Middle East.

Soak the bulgur wheat in cold water for 1 hour. Drain well and put into a large serving bowl with all remaining ingredients. Season generously and toss.

☼ May be prepared earlier in the day.

Cook's tip: To save time, chop the herbs in a food processor first, then use it for the mango mixture without washing it up in between – a few left-over herbs won't hurt.

MANGETOUT AND BABY TOMATOES IN A MUSTARD VINAIGRETTE

500g (1lb 2oz) mangetout

500g (1lb 2oz) cherry tomatoes

6 tbsp ready-made French dressing (M & S Lite French Dressing recommended)

3 tsp grain mustard

The mustard gives these crunchy vegetables a real zing.

Top and tail the mangetout. Put in a bowl, pour boiling water over them, leave for one minute, drain and rinse in cold water. Arrange around the edge of a large serving platter or bowl. Cut tomatoes in half and arrange in the middle. Mix French dressing with mustard and pour over the salad.

Cook's tip: If you are pushed for time, buy ready topped and tailed mangetout (available in most large supermarkets) and leave the tomatoes whole – they don't look quite as impressive but still look pretty good.

ICED LEMON TERRINE WITH A BOOZY BLUEBERRY COULIS

12 tbsp crunch nut cornflakes, frosties or similar cereal

300ml (½pt) double cream

500g (1lb 2oz) Greek yoghurt

1 jar (400g) lemon curd

COULIS

170g (6oz) blueberries

slug cassis, framboise, Cointreau or other fruity liqueur (approx. 4 tbsp or more)

1 tbsp icing sugar

A lovely refreshing dessert for a warm summers evening.

Line a terrine or loaf tin with foil. Roughly crush the cornflakes and put half in the bottom of the tin. Whip the cream until stiff and fold in the yoghurt and lemon curd. Spread in tin on top of crushed cornflakes and sprinkle remaining ones on top. Cover and freeze for at least 2½ hours.

To make coulis – blend all ingredients in a food processor or liquidize.

◗ ❊ May be prepared up to this point the day before. As well as the terrine, the coulis may also be frozen.

To serve – take terrine out of freezer about 15 minutes before serving. Turn out onto a serving dish and remove foil. Slice and serve with coulis.

Cook's tip: If you're like me, you will probably forget to take the terrine out of the freezer 15 minutes before serving. It will be rock hard but you can pacify yourself by the fact that we're all the same.

The day before:
1. Make terrine and coulis.
2. Prepare mango chicken up to ◗.

Earlier on the day:
3. Make tabbouleh.
4. Prepare mangetout.

In the evening:
5. Finish preparing mango chicken.
6. Make mangetout and tomato salad.
7. Make starter.

ORDER OF PREPARATION IN UNDER 2 HOURS:
1. Make terrine and coulis and hope that by the time you have eaten everything else, it will be frozen!
2. Make tabbouleh.
3. Make mango chicken.
4. Make mangetout and tomato salad.
5. Make starter.

SIMPLY SPANISH

Spanish dishes vary a great deal from region to region. These Spanish-style recipes are not necessarily authentic but are so incredibly easy that you can cook them and remain relaxed enough to feel you are on holiday in Spain. You will get the authentic "Mañana" feeling!

TAPAS – GARLIC MUSHROOMS, CHORIZO AND OLIVES
EASY PAELLA
AVOCADO AND PALM HEART SALAD
LEMON SURPRISE RAMEKINS

♀ *Soft Spanish red.*
Recommendation – Vega Sindoa
Crianza from Spain

TAPAS

These are a selection of nibbles to eat with drinks – traditionally sherry. In Spain they sometimes make a complete meal of them.

GARLIC MUSHROOMS

500g (1lb 2oz) button mushrooms
3 garlic cloves – crushed
6 tbsp olive oil
2 tbsp balsamic vinegar
salt and pepper
cocktail sticks

Wipe mushrooms clean and mix with other ingredients. Serve with cocktail sticks.

☼ These are better prepared earlier in the day to allow them time to marinate.

CHORIZO

500g (1lb 2oz) chorizo

This can either be bought as a long thin sausage or as a shorter fat sausage, rather like salami. If you buy the short fat type, get a large chunk and don't get it sliced.

Remove the tough outer skin then cut it into bite-sized chunks. Serve with cocktail sticks.

OLIVES

400g (14oz) olives

Choose any of the many varieties and styles now available.

EASY PAELLA

| 2 tbsp olive oil |
| 1 large onion – chopped |
| 2 garlic cloves – crushed |
| 1 tsp paprika |
| 1 tsp turmeric |
| 450g (1lb) long-grain rice |
| 1.2 litres (2pts) chicken or fish stock – made with 2 stock cubes and boiling water |
| 4 tomatoes – chopped |
| 1 red pepper – de-seeded and chopped |
| 4 ready-cooked chicken breasts – skinned and chopped |
| 500g (1lb 2oz) ready-to-eat seafood cocktail – fresh or frozen and de-frosted |
| 24 fresh mussels in shells or large prawns in shells (see "Cook's tip" right) |
| 100g (3½oz) frozen peas |
| 2 lemons – cut into wedges |
| salt and pepper |

The beauty of this recipe is that most of it can be prepared in advance, leaving just the minimum to do at the last minute. Don't be put off by the long list of ingredients. It's very easy and is a meal within itself. For a change I have used turmeric rather than the more traditional saffron. You ideally need a large paella pan for this recipe, but a wok will work just as well.

Heat oil and gently fry onions and garlic for about 3 minutes. Stir in paprika, turmeric and rice and cook for a further 3 minutes. Add stock.

☼ May be prepared up to this point earlier in the day.

The remaining ingredients may also be prepared so that all you have to do is add them to the pan. See "Cook's tip" below for instructions on how to prepare mussels.

Bring rice and stock mixture up to the boil and allow to simmer, uncovered, for 10 minutes. Add tomatoes, peppers, chicken, seafood cocktail, mussels and frozen peas and cook for a further 10 minutes, stirring regularly, until rice has absorbed all the liquid. Season and serve with lemon wedges.

Cook's tip: Fresh mussels look good with the paella and give it a real authentic feel. They must be as fresh as possible, bought on the day or the day before eaten. To prepare them, scrub under cold running water to remove all grit and remove beards. The mussels should be tightly closed before cooking and you should discard any which remain open when tapped. This can be done earlier in the day and they can be left to soak in water until needed. Once the mussels are cooked, the shells should open and they should be discarded if they don't. If you think this sounds like a real hassle, then substitute the mussels for large prawns in shells which can be bought fresh or frozen.

AVOCADO AND PALM HEART SALAD

| 200g bag mixed salad leaves |
| 2 large ripe avocados – peeled and sliced |
| ½ lemon |
| 1 tin (400g) palm hearts – drained and sliced |
| 8 tbsp ready-made French dressing (M & S Lite recommended) |

Palm hearts have a very delicate and quite exquisite taste. They make this salad really interesting and different.

Put leaves onto a large platter or flattish bowl. Squeeze juice of lemon over avocado slices to stop them going black and arrange with palm hearts on top of leaves. Pour over dressing and serve.

Cook's tip: If you can't find palm hearts, use tinned artichokes instead.

Opposite: "And Here's One I Made Earlier" (page 103)

LEMON SURPRISE RAMEKINS

300ml (½pt) double cream

500g (1lb 2oz) fromage frais

1 jar (400g) lemon curd

1 packet tuiles amandes biscuits or other biscuits

A demon dessert but your guests will think you spent hours zesting and squeezing lemons.

Whisk cream and fold in fromage frais and lemon curd. Put in ramekin dishes and chill in fridge for at least 1 hour.

❂ May be made the day before or may be frozen.

Serve chilled with tuiles amandes.

Cook's tip: Leave a piece of lemon rind and a zester lying around to make this dessert look authentic!

ORDER OF PREPARATION IF
MAKING IN ADVANCE:

The day before:
1. Make lemon ramekins.

Earlier on the day:
2. Make garlic mushrooms.
3. Make paella up to ❂ and prepare remaining ingredients.

In the evening:
4. Prepare tapas.
5. Prepare salad and dress before serving.
7. Finish off paella.

ORDER OF PREPARATION IN
UNDER 2 HOURS:
1. Make lemon ramekins.
2. Make garlic mushrooms.
3. Prepare paella up to ❂ prepare other ingredients and continue cooking as needed.
4. Make other tapas.
5. Prepare salad.

Opposite: Totally Vegetarian (page 150)

SUNSET ON MONT BLANC

Mont Blanc is the mountain which separates France from Italy. There is a tunnel running through the mountain which joins the two countries. This menu is a real mixture of French / Italian cooking. While creating the recipes, I could imagine having aperitifs and the starter in Italy overlooking the "Monte Bianco" (as it is known on the Italian side), driving into France for the main course and dessert and slipping back into Italy for a quick Sambucca and espresso.

♀ *French Chardonnay.*
Recommendation – St Veran, Cuvèe Prestige, Roger Lassarat

MINI PIZZETTAS WITH ARTICHOKE, FETA AND TOMATO
SWORDFISH STEAKS NIÇOISE WITH MARINATED VEGETABLES
CARROT, CORIANDER AND LIME SALAD
NEW POTATOES
SUMMER FRUIT AND CASSIS SYLLABUB WITH BRANDYSNAP BISCUITS

MINI PIZZETTAS WITH ARTICHOKE, FETA AND TOMATO

1 packet "French Experience" 4 mini baguettes (bread dough)

100g (3½oz) tomato purée

6 tomatoes – sliced and ends discarded

1 tin (400g) artichoke hearts – drained and cut into quarters

200g (7oz) feta cheese

100g packet mixed salad leaves

6 tbsp ready-made French dressing

Oven: 200ºC, 400ºF, Gas Mark 6

These individual pizza type starters are made beautifully light by using ready-made bread dough. The artichokes and feta combine well to give a distinctive taste, though other toppings may be used instead.

Unwrap baguettes and separate into 4 along perforated lines. Cut each one in half to form 8 squares, slightly stretch out and place on a baking tray. Spread tomato purée on each one, followed by sliced tomatoes and artichoke quarters. Finish off with feta crumbled on top.

☀ May be prepared up to this point earlier in the day.

Put in oven for 15-20 minutes and serve with mixed salad leaves and dressing drizzled over.

Cook's tip: If you have problems finding the ready-made bread dough, use mini pitta rounds instead as a base.

SWORDFISH STEAKS NIÇOISE WITH MARINATED VEGETABLES

8 swordfish steaks

1 jar (approx 285g) mixed peppers in oil

1 jar (approx 290g) "Condiverdi" with Mediterranean Vegetables, or a tomato-based pasta sauce may be used instead

2 garlic cloves – crushed

1 small tin pitted black olives –drained

2 lemons

salt and pepper

Oven: 200ºC, 400ºF, Gas Mark 6

This is one of the quickest and simplest recipes you could hope to find, yet sumptuously full of delicate flavours.

Place swordfish steaks in an oven-proof dish in one layer. Pour contents of jars on top and mix in crushed garlic and olives. Season and cover with foil.

◗ May be prepared up to this point the day before.

Cook in oven for 30 minutes.

Cut lemons into wedges and serve with swordfish.

Cook's tip: Other fish may be used instead, e.g. tuna, shark, monkfish.

CARROT, CORIANDER AND LIME SALAD

1 handful fresh chopped coriander

1 handful fresh chopped parsley

8 spring onions – sliced

1kg (2lbs 4oz) carrots

1 lime

6 tbsp olive oil

1 tsp sugar

salt and pepper

A lovely fresh salad full of flavours and colours.

Chop the coriander and parsley in a food processor first and mix in a large salad bowl with sliced spring onions. Peel and thinly slice carrots, preferably in a food processor, and mix with herbs.

To make dressing – mix together zest and juice of lime, olive oil, sugar and seasoning. Pour over carrots and herbs and toss.

☼ May be prepared earlier in the day.

Cook's tip: This salad can be varied by grating the carrots.

NEW POTATOES

1.5kg (3lbs 5oz) new potatoes

salt and pepper

Plain boiled new potatoes are the only thing that goes well and does not compete with all the flavours of the other recipes.

Wash potatoes, put into boiling water and simmer for 10-15 minutes. Season and serve.

Cook's tip: Buy a new season's new potato like Jersey Royals which are firm and full of flavour.

SUMMER FRUIT AND CASSIS SYLLABUB WITH BRANDYSNAP BISCUITS

300ml (½pt) double or whipping cream

2 level tbsp icing sugar

large slug cassis

400ml (14oz) carton ready - made custard – preferably fresh but long-life will do

500g (1lb 2oz) frozen summer fruit – de-frosted and drained

1 packet brandysnaps or 8 brandysnap baskets

A wonderfully seductive syllabub. The brandysnap biscuits are a real cheat but are sure to impress your friends and convince them that they took hours to make.

Whisk cream with icing sugar and cassis until thick. Fold in custard and summer fruits.

Put into a serving dish or individual ramekins and chill for at least 1 hour. To make brandysnap biscuits – line a baking tray with baking parchment, place brandysnaps/baskets on top with enough room around them to spread out and put in oven: 190°C, 375°F, Gas Mark 5 for 3 minutes. Alternatively, put individually in a microwave on baking parchment on high for 30–40 seconds each. Take out of oven/microwave, uncurl if necessary, flatten out and leave to cool. Serve with syllabub.

◗ ❄ May be made the day before or may be frozen. Serve chilled.

Cook's tip: The timing of the brandysnaps is crucial as they can burn easily.

ORDER OF PREPARATION IF MAKING IN ADVANCE:

The day before:
1. Make syllabub and brandysnap biscuits.
2. Prepare swordfish up to ◗

Earlier on the day:
3. Prepare pizzettas up to ❄
4. Make carrot and coriander salad.

In the evening:
5. Cook pizzettas as needed.
6. Put swordfish in oven.
7. Cook new potatoes.

ORDER OF PREPARATION IN UNDER 2 HOURS:
1. Make syllabub and brandysnap biscuits.
2. Prepare swordfish and cook as needed.
3. Prepare pizzettas and cook as needed.
4. Make carrot and coriander salad.
5. Cook potatoes as needed.

Autumn

AUTUMN FRUIT PLATTER

Choose three of the following fruits and arrange on a large platter.

FIGS (dried)

FIGS (fresh) – cut in quarters

GRAPES (black or white) – cut into little bunches of 8-10

MANGO – peeled, stone removed and sliced

MELON – sliced and skin removed

PASSION FRUIT – cut in half

PERSIMMON (Sharon Fruit) – cut in quarters

A CHINESE EXPERIENCE

As a special treat when I was a child, my parents would order a take away from our local Chinese restaurant. We always ordered the same thing – "Menu 3" – as my Mother was convinced that "Menus 1 and 2" had stir-fried alsatian and mice tails in them! Menu 3 included the statutory spare ribs, sweet and sour pork, chicken chow mein, special fried rice and lychees. We would rush back from the restaurant with our cardboard and polystyrene containers and put them in the oven to bring out individually when needed. We often found at the end of the meal we were left with one warm, melting polystyrene container and couldn't guess what it was until we remembered that we hadn't eaten the lychees yet!

These days Chinese cooking has become so much more sophisticated but can be very time consuming to prepare. As one Chinese cookery book said "allow plenty of time for preparation as many dishes just do not allow time to turn around and scramble amid a chaos of half-prepared ingredients". The following recipes may not be truly authentic, but they are extremely quick to prepare and do allow you time to "scramble" without chaos.

A rich ripe white and a Pinot Noir. Recommendations – Pinot Blanc 'Cuvée Caroline', Schoffit, Alsace ... and Sterling Redwood ... Pinot Noir from California

WARM SCALLOP SALAD

DUCK BREASTS WITH WATER CHESTNUTS IN A PLUM AND FIVE SPICE SAUCE

TIMBALES OF WILD RICE AND CORIANDER

MANGETOUT, COURGETTE AND LEEK STIR-FRY

LYCHEES WITH GINGER ICE CREAM AND GINGER WINE

WARM SCALLOP SALAD

16 large scallops
1 red pepper – de-seeded and sliced
8 spring onions – thickly sliced on the diagonal
3cm (1¼") cube fresh root ginger – finely chopped
2 garlic cloves – chopped or crushed
1 red chilli – de-seeded and finely chopped or a few drops of chilli sauce (optional)
4 tbsp soy sauce
juice of 1 lemon
2 tbsp olive oil
100g bag mixed salad leaves
salt and pepper

Scallops are very popular with the Chinese. They are best cooked quickly as they become tough when over-cooked. In some recipes they are served barely cooked, but I find them rather "slimy" and prefer them cooked through.

Clean the scallops (see Cook's tip below), separate and retain the corals. Slice the scallops in half horizontally. Mix together in a bowl with the corals, red pepper, spring onions, ginger, garlic, chilli, soy sauce, lemon juice, salt and pepper. Leave to marinate for at least 1 hour.

☀ May be prepared up to this point earlier in the day.

Heat the oil in a frying pan or wok. Add scallop mixture and fry over a high heat for 5-7 minutes, until the scallops are cooked through.

To serve – arrange mixed salad leaves on individual plates and put scallop mixture on top. Serve with warm bread – see Handy Hints page 6.

Cook's tip: Scallops are quite often sold with the muscular white frill found opposite the coral (orange roe) already removed. If not, you should remove and discard it before cooking.

DUCK BREASTS WITH WATER CHESTNUTS IN A PLUM AND FIVE SPICE SAUCE

8 duck breasts
2 tins (225g each) water chestnuts – drained and sliced
1 jar (approx. 250g–300g) plum sauce
4 tsp Chinese Five Spice
4 tbsp dry sherry
Oven: 230ºC, 450ºF, Gas Mark 8

For over 2000 years the Chinese have been breeding duck for food and have considered it a symbol of wholesomeness and fidelity.
Unfortunately, duck has rather a lot of fat and bones and can be difficult to serve for a dinner party. In this recipe I have used only the breasts with the skin removed so that it is neither fatty nor bony and is easy to serve.

Remove skin and fat from duck breasts. Mix sliced water chestnuts, plum sauce, Chinese Five Spice and sherry together in a large bowl and add duck. This can be left to marinate until needed.

☀ May be prepared up to this point earlier in the day.

Put into a roasting dish and cook in oven for approximately 20 minutes (cook for less if you like duck pink inside and more if you like it better cooked).

To serve – thinly slice each duck breast, fan out on each plate and spoon over sauce.

Cook's tip: Slicing the duck can be a bit of a pain as you h___ do it at the last minute, but it looks so impressive that it is well worth the e___ t.

MANGETOUT, COURGETTE AND LEEK STIR-FRY

2 tbsp sesame or olive oil

4 leeks – sliced on the diagonal

4 courgettes – sliced on the diagonal

200g (7oz) mangetout – topped and tailed

3 tbsp soy sauce

salt and pepper

These three green vegetables look very effective together.

Heat oil in a wok and add vegetables. Stir-fry for 2 minutes, add soy sauce and continue for another 5 minutes. Season and serve.

Cook's tip: As these are so quick to cook, I suggest you stir-fry them after the first course. They taste so much better when they are freshly cooked and crisp and can be served directly out of the wok.

TIMBALES OF WILD RICE AND CORIANDER

400g (14oz) mixed long-grain and wild rice

1 handful chopped coriander

salt and pepper

You can now buy packets of mixed long-grain and wild rice. The timbales look incredibly impressive and are so easy to make.

Cook rice according to instructions on packet. Drain if necessary and mix with coriander, salt and pepper. Pack tightly into 8 warmed ramekin dishes and turn out on to serving plates.

Cook's tip: If you prefer not to make the timbales, the duck can be served fanned out on top of a bed of rice.

LYCHEES WITH GINGER ICE CREAM AND GINGER WINE

1 litre good quality vanilla ice cream

1 jar (440g) stem ginger in syrup

slug ginger wine (approx 4 tbsp) – optional

2 tins (425g) lychees

The Chinese are not too hot on desserts but this ice cream is wonderfully refreshing to finish off the meal.

Allow ice cream to soften slightly. Drain stem ginger, reserving syrup, and roughly chop. Mix chopped ginger with ice cream and return to freezer for at least 2 hours. Mix syrup with ginger wine.

❶ ❋ May be made up to this point the day before and the ice cream may be kept in the freezer for a few months.

To serve – drain lychees and combine with ice cream and ginger wine syrup.

Cook's tip: This ice cream also goes well with sliced mango.

ORDER OF PREPARATION IF MAKING IN ADVANCE:

1. Make ice cream and ginger wine sauce.

   Earlier on the day:
2. Prepare scallop salad up to ❋
3. Prepare duck up to ❋

   In the evening:
4. Prepare vegetables ready to stir-fry.
5. Cook duck as needed.
6. Cook rice as needed.
7. Cook scallops as needed.
8. Stir-fry vegetables.

ORDER OF PREPARATION IN UNDER 2 HOURS:

1. Make ice cream and ginger wine sauce.
2. Prepare duck and cook as needed.
3. Prepare scallops and cook as needed.
4. Cook rice when needed.
5. Stir-fry vegetables.

COLOURS OF AUTUMN

This is a lovely menu to serve when the weather is beginning to get colder and evenings are getting darker. The warm autumn colours in these recipes, including the red cabbage, orange of the sweet potatoes, golden pastry and the rich dark chocolate soufflé cake, ease you into the approaching winter.

ROQUEFORT STUFFED MUSHROOMS
LAMB CUTLETS EN CROUTE WITH A REDCURRANT SAUCE
PARSLEYED SWEET POTATOES
RED CABBAGE WITH ORANGE
CHOCOLATE SOUFFLÉ CAKE WITH MOCHA BEANS AND A "BAILEYS" SAUCE

A rich ripe new world Grenache. Recommendations – Peter Lehmann, Grenache from Australia

ROQUEFORT-STUFFED MUSHROOMS

The inspiration for this recipe came from my friend Rebecca. She had been making these stuffed mushrooms for her Directors lunches and couldn't believe how something so simple could get so many compliments.

8 very large flat mushrooms
225g (8oz) Roquefort
2 little gem lettuces – shredded
Oven: 200°C, 400°F, Gas Mark 6

Wipe the mushrooms with a damp cloth to remove dirt and remove stalks. Crumble the Roquefort and divide between the mushrooms.

❊ May be prepared earlier in the day.

Either put on a baking tray in oven for 15 minutes, or put under a hot grill for 5 minutes until Roquefort is bubbling. Serve on a bed of shredded lettuce and warm crusty bread – see Handy Hints page 6.

Cook's tip: Roquefort is quite delicious and goes exceptionally well with the mushrooms but tends to be rather expensive. If you don't want to be so extravagant use Stilton or Danish Blue instead.

LAMB CUTLETS EN CROUTE WITH A REDCURRANT SAUCE

These take a little more time to prepare but once you have done the first, the remaining ones will seem quick and easy. It is well worth the effort as the finished effect is so mega impressive.

3 racks of lamb or 16 lamb cutlets – (ask butcher to separate, trim and cut off the fat and meat around the tips of the bone)
10g (¼oz) butter
1 tbsp olive oil
500g (2 x 250g) ready-made puff pastry
1 jar (approx 300g) redcurrant jelly
1 egg – beaten
1 carton (284ml / ½pt) fresh concentrated beef stock
4 tbsp port
salt and pepper
Oven: 200°C, 400°F, Gas Mark 6

Separate cutlets and trim off any remaining fat. Melt butter and ... ving pan and quickly brown the cutlets (approximately 20 seconds ... Leave to cool.

... pastry thinly, cut each one into 4 squ... square into ... to make 16 triangles. Spread a thin ... jelly on each cu... season. Place ...ch of the cutlets o... pastry, dampe... with water ...d wrap over the cutle... Use any left ... pas... immings to decorate the cutlets. Brush with bu...

To make sauce – mix beef stock, port and remaining redcurrant jelly together in a saucepan.

☀ All the above may be prepared up to this point earlier in the day.

Brush a baking tray with oil and heat in oven for a few minutes. Put cutlets on to the hot tray and cook for 20 minutes.

Bring sauce to boil and allow to simmer gently for 20 minutes.

Cook's tip: For decoration, use a very small pastry cutter to cut out shapes. Damp the bottom of the pastry shape with water and put it on top of the cutlet. I have a small heart shape which I often use – it's ideal for Valentine's night.

RED CABBAGE WITH ORANGE

1 large red cabbage
1 large onion – thinly sliced
1 carton frozen concentrated orange juice
3 tsp caraway seeds
salt and pepper

A very healthy vegetable dish with no added butter or oil. The caraway seeds give the cabbage a slight aniseed flavour.

Cut red cabbage into quarters, cut away the core and shred crossways. Put into a large saucepan with all the remaining ingredients. Cover the pan and cook gently for 1½ hours, stirring occasionally.

◗ ☀ May be made in advance or frozen.

To re-heat – either put in a microwave on high for 7 minutes, stirring half way through, or put in the oven: 190°C, 375°F, Gas mark 5 for 30 minutes.

Cook's tip: I often double this recipe and freeze half. Red cabbage is one of the few vegetables which tastes just as good the second time round.

PARSLEYED SWEET POTATO

1.5kg (3lbs 5oz) sweet potatoes
25g (1oz) butter or "Olivio"
bunch parsley – chopped
salt and pepper

The orangey colour and sweetness of these potatoes make a pleasant change from the normal white potato.

Peel sweet potatoes, cut into cubes (approximately 1cm / ½") and put immediately into a saucepan of water to stop discolouring. Add a pinch of salt. Bring water to the boil and simmer for 15-20 minutes or until potatoes are tender. Drain, return to the pan, add remaining ingredients and toss over a gentle heat for a few seconds.

Cook's tip: The flesh of sweet potatoes can be orange or yellow in colour. Try and buy the orange ones as they don't discolour so easily.

CHOCOLATE SOUFFLÉ CAKE WITH MOCHA BEANS AND A "BAILEYS" SAUCE

300g (11oz) dark chocolate
large slug Baileys (approx 4 tbsp)
6 eggs
175g (6oz) castor sugar
100g (3½oz) chocolate coated coffee beans
1 tbsp icing sugar
SAUCE
150ml (¼pt) single cream
150ml (¼pt) carton ready-made custard
Oven: 190ºC, 375ºF, Gas Mark 5

This soufflé cake will rise during cooking and then sink dramatically as it cools. Throwing some coffee beans on top and then sprinkling over icing sugar gives it an interesting finished appearance – something like 'golf balls in the snow'. When I served this pudding at a dinner party, it was described by one guest as quite "orgasmic". You'll have your guests begging for more!

Grease a round spring-form or loose-bottomed cake tin – approximate size 24cm (9½") in diameter. Melt the chocolate with 2 tbsp Baileys either over a pan of simmering water or in a microwave on medium for 3-4 minutes. Meanwhile, separate the eggs and whisk the whites until stiff. Whisk the yolks with the castor sugar until it becomes pale. Whisk the melted chocolate into the yolks and fold in the whites and half the coffee beans. Put into cake tin and cook for 25 minutes. Leave to cool but don't panic when the cake begins to sink – this is meant to happen.

To make sauce – mix cream, custard and remaining Baileys together.

❂ ❋ May be made up to this point the day before and the soufflé cake may be frozen and serve chilled.

To serve – remove side of cake tin. Put remaining coffee beans on top of cake and sieve icing sugar over the top. Serve with sauce.

Cook's tip: The amount of Baileys you add to the sauce is a matter of taste – the more the merrier. While on the subject of tasting, it's very tempting to do a lot, but make sure you have some sauce left to serve with the soufflé!

ORDER OF PREPARATION IF MAKING IN ADVANCE:

The day before:
1. Make red cabbage with orange.
2. Make soufflé cake up to ❋

Earlier on the day:
3. Prepare stuffed mushrooms.
4. Prepare lamb en croûte up to ❋

In the evening:
5. Peel sweet potatoes and leave in cold water until ready to cook.
6. Re-heat red cabbage.
7. Cook lamb en croûte as necessary and heat sauce.
8. Finish off soufflé cake.
9. Heat mushrooms and bread.

ORDER OF PREPARATION IN UNDER 2 HOURS:
1. Make soufflé cake.
2. Make red cabbage with orange.
3. Prepare lamb en croûte and cook as necessary.
4. Cook sweet potatoes.
5. Make stuffed mushrooms and heat bread.

FONDUE WITH A DIFFERENCE

Fondues conjure up images of burning oil, stringy cheese and indigestion but a fondue Chinoise is something completely different. The difference is that you use a selection of different meats that are cooked in a broth rather than oil. This makes the meal far healthier and safer from a fire risk. Fondues are ideal when inviting friends who don't know each other – they are a very sociable meal. They are also very useful for people with little babies – you can leave the table and feed the baby while everyone does their own cooking.

MINI TARTLETTES OF LEEK, BACON AND CAMBOZOLA

FONDUE CHINOISE WITH DIPS (LAMB, CHICKEN, PORK AND BEEF COOKED IN A BOUILLON WITH WILD MUSHROOMS)

SPINACH, LETTUCE AND HAZELNUT SALAD WITH A HONEYED HAZELNUT DRESSING

ROAST POTATO WEDGES

BOUILLON SOUP

CAPPUCCINO MOUSSE AU FAVORITE

♀ A fruity New World red. Recommendation – Errazuriz Merlot from Chile

MINI TARTLETTES OF LEEK, BACON AND CAMBOZOLA

As you seem to be sitting down at the table for a long time eating fondues, this starter is ideal to serve with drinks.

Roll out each slice of bread with a rolling pin to make them slightly larger and thinner. With a round pastry cutter (approximately 6cm / 2½" in diameter) cut two rounds out of each slice of bread. Push the 24 rounds into tart tins and lightly brush with olive oil. Put in oven for 15 minutes until golden.

◗ May be made up to 2 days before and kept in an air-tight container.

Heat 1 tbsp olive oil in a large frying pan, add bacon and fry until golden. Add leeks and continue frying until leeks have softened. Divide leek and bacon mixture between tarts. Thinly slice Cambozola, including the outside rind, and place a slice on top of each tart.

☼ May be prepared up to this point earlier in the day.

Put back in oven for 10-15 minutes until cheese has melted.

Cook's tips: Serving the tarts with drinks, means you don't need the extra cutlery and plates and save on washing up. The left over bread and crusts can be used to make breadcrumbs and kept in the freezer until needed.

12 slices brown bread (thin or medium sliced)
olive oil
175g (6oz) streaky, rindless bacon – chopped
3 medium leeks – thinly sliced
175g (6oz) Cambozola
Oven: 190ºC, 375ºF, Gas Mark 5

FONDUE CHINOISE

350g (12oz) rump steak –
cut into thin strips

350g (12oz) pork fillet –
cut into thin strips

350g (12oz) diced leg of lamb

350g (12oz) chicken breasts –
cut into thin strips

1.2 litres (2 pts) water

2 chicken stock cubes

4 cartons (284ml/½pt each)
fresh concentrated chicken stock

40g (1½oz) dried wild mushrooms
(e.g. ceps, porcini, etc) – washed

slug of medium or dry sherry
(approx 4tbsp)

DIPS

Mustard Mayonnaise – 1 bottle
(340ml) Dijonnaise

Garlic Mayonnaise – 5 tbsp
mayonnaise mixed with 2 garlic
cloves – crushed

Tomato Salsa – 1 jar (approx
226g) mild salsa – "Pace"
recommended + 1 chopped tomato
mixed with it

Curry Dip – 1 small pot (150g)
yoghurt, 2 tbsp mayonnaise, 2 tbsp
mango chutney and 2 tsp curry
powder mixed together

This method of cooking meat in a broth is far healthier than using oil and by the time all the meat has cooked in it, the flavours have infused and it is served as the most wonderful soup.

There are 4 different dips. Divide each one between two ramekin dishes, allowing one set of dips for each end of the table. Arrange sliced meat on two large plates for people to help themselves.

☼ May be prepared up to this point earlier in the day.

Boil water in a large saucepan and stir in chicken stock cubes to dissolve. Add cartons of stock and dried mushrooms. Heat gently and allow to simmer for 30 minutes.

You will require two fondue sets, one from each end of the table, which you will need to light. Pour stock into fondue bowls and allow to simmer. Give each guest a fondue fork and let them cook their own meat and help themselves to dips.

When everyone has finished, pour sherry into stock and serve as soup.

Cook's tip: To make the evening fun, announce that if anyone looses a piece of meat in the fondue bowl, they should be made to do a forfeit, e.g. take an item of clothing off, recite a poem, sing a song…

SPINACH, LETTUCE AND HAZELNUT SALAD WITH A HONEYED HAZELNUT DRESSING

100g (3½oz) hazelnuts

200g baby spinach leaves – you
can buy them in packets ready-
washed

1 cos lettuce or other crisp
lettuce, e.g. iceberg, little gem –
washed, drained and sliced

DRESSING

8 tbsp hazelnut oil

2 tbsp balsamic vinegar

2 tsp runny honey

salt and pepper

This simple salad is perfect to serve with a fondue. The dressing gives it the most wonderful subtle flavour of hazelnuts.

Put hazelnuts under a hot grill until golden. Mix in a large salad bowl with spinach and lettuce. Mix all dressing ingredients together, pour over salad, toss and serve.

Cook's tip: This salad can be varied by using walnuts and walnut oil instead of hazelnut.

ROAST POTATO WEDGES

1.5 kg (3lbs) large potatoes

2 tbsp olive oil

salt and pepper

Oven: 200°C, 400°F, Gas Mark 6

These are similar to the deep-fried potato skins that you often find in American restaurants, but are even better. I have been known to call them "classy chips".

Scrub potatoes and cut each one into 6-8 into wedges. Put the oil in a large roasting dish in the oven to heat for a few minutes. Add potato wedges, season generously and toss in oil. Cook for 1½ hours, tossing occasionally.

Cook's tip: If you want to save time, buy frozen potato skins, available from most large supermarkets, which can be baked in the oven.

CAPPUCCINO MOUSSE AU FAVORITE

275ml (½ pt) very strong black coffee

1 sachet (11g) gelatine

4 heaped tbsp sugar – granulated or castor

300ml (½ pt) double cream

250g (9oz) Mascarpone

500ml (18fl oz) carton ready-made custard– preferable fresh but long-life will do

large slug liqueur (approx. 4 tbsp or as much as you dare!) – Baileys recommended but others will be just as good, e.g. brandy, whisky, Tia Maria

1 tbsp chocolate or cocoa power

1 packet chocolate coated coffee beans or approx 50g (2oz)

An irresistible dessert which is always a real favourite. It is quite rich so you need only give each person a small amount. It looks good served in either small coffee cups or wine glasses.

Make coffee and while piping hot, add gelatine and sugar. Stir until both have dissolved and allow to cool.

Reserve 3 tbsp of the cream and whisk the rest until stiff. Add Mascarpone and custard and gently whisk (don't panic if it is slightly lumpy). Add liqueur and cooled coffee and whisk briefly to blend. Pour into cups or glasses and put in fridge for at least 1 hour to set.

◗ ❋ May be made up to this point the day before or may be frozen and serve chilled.

Pour remaining cream on top of mousses. Put a few chocolate coated coffee beans on top and finish off with sieved chocolate powder.

Cook's tip: The trick to using gelatine successfully, is to make sure that it is virtually the same temperature as the mixture which you are going to add it to. Failure to do this will make it go stringy.

ORDER OF PREPARATION IF MAKING IN ADVANCE:

The day before:
1. Make cappuccino mousses up to ❋
2. Make mini tartlettes up to ◗
3. Make dressing for salad.

Earlier on the day:
4. Make dips for fondue and prepare meat up to ☼

In the evening:
5. Finish off cappuccino mousses.
6. Prepare and cook roast potato wedges.
7. Finish off preparations for fondue.
8. Prepare salad but do not toss in dressing until just before serving.
. Put tartlettes in oven to warm.

ORDER OF PREPARATION IN UNDER 2 HOURS:
1. Make cappuccino mousses up to ❋ and finish off just before serving.
2. Prepare and cook roast potato wedges.
3. Prepare fondue and dips, start bouillon and light fondue sets when necessary.
4. Make tarts.
5. Prepare salad.

CELERIAC AND LEEK PURÉE

2 medium celeriac

6 large leeks

2 garlic cloves

2 tbsp olive oil

1 tsp sugar

salt and pepper

1 tbsp chopped parsley

Celeriac is not regularly used in this country. Don't be put off by its ugly appearance, it has a wonderful flavour and goes well with the leeks in this purée. You may need to tell your guests what it is as they probably won't know.

Peel and dice celeriac. Put into water immediately to prevent discolouring. Wash leeks, slice and add to celeriac. Bring water up to the boil and allow to simmer for approximately 15 minutes until vegetables are very soft. Drain. Put the garlic in a food processor to chop. Add leek and celeriac mixture, olive oil, sugar, salt and pepper (this may need to be done in batches).

◗ ❋ May be made up to this point the day before and may be frozen at this stage but must be left to cool before putting in freezer.

To re-heat – de-frost and either put in bowl and microwave on high for 7 minutes, stirring half way through or put in oven: 190ºC, 375ºF, Gas Mark 5 for 20 minutes covered with foil. Sprinkle chopped parsley on top.

Cook's tip: When cooking the celeriac and leeks, make sure they are very soft before draining them. This will make them easier for you to purée.

CARAMEL CRUNCH SURPRISE

300ml (½pt) double or whipping cream

3 chocolate "Crunchie" bars

3 muesli bars

chocolate wafer biscuits

I made up this recipe when working as a "Chalet Girl". It's so quick that I could be out on the slopes early in the morning.

Crunch up "Crunchie" and muesli bars into small pieces. Whisk cream until stiff and fold in crunchie mixture. Put in 8 ramekin dishes and freeze for at least 1 hour.

❋ May be frozen.

Take out of freezer 10 minutes before serving and serve with chocolate wafer biscuits.

Cooks tip: Don't eat too many pieces of "Crunchie" while you make this!

ORDER OF PREPARATION IF
MAKING IN ADVANCE:

To put in the freezer:
1. Make soup up to ❋
2. Prepare stuffed plaice up to ❋
3. Prepare potato dauphinoise up to ❋
4. Make leek and celeriac purée up to ❋
5. Make caramel crunch surprise.

ORDER OF PREPARATION IN
UNDER 2 HOURS:
1. Make potatoes dauphinoise and cook.
2. Make caramel crunch surprise and put in freezer.
3. Make leek and celeriac purée and re-heat before serving if necessary.
4. Make soup.
5. Prepare stuffed plaice and cook as needed.

Opposite: Sunset On Mont Blanc (page 82)

FEELING FRENCH

French cuisine is the best in the world, or so the French would say. They devote a huge amount of time each day to thinking about food, agonising over menus, cooking and eating. French cooking varies from region to region and from haute cuisine to the more simple, rustic food. Haute cuisine and nouvelle cuisine can take an absurd amount of time to concoct and virtually requires an architectural plan to present.

In this menu I have used a mixture of dishes from different regions and styles. The French love their tarts, so I have started with a sophisticated three pepper tart, followed by cassoulet, real French peasant food, and finishing with a light refreshing vacherin (meringue) piled high with strawberry ice cream and summer fruits. No planning permission will be required for any of these recipes!

THREE PEPPER TART
QUICK CASSOULET WITH GARLIC BREAD
BABY SPINACH LEAF SALAD WITH A WALNUT AND RASPBERRY VINAIGRETTE
VACHERIN GLACÉ WITH SUMMER FRUITS AND CASSIS

♀ Southern French Red. Recommendation – Costières de Nimes, Domaine Mas Carlot

THREE PEPPER TART

This is a lovely colourful tart using three different colours of pepper. Red peppers are a riper version of the green ones but the yellow ones are a different strain altogether.

1 packet (350g) ready-rolled puff pastry (see Cook's tip below)
2 tbsp olive oil
1 green, yellow and red pepper – de-seeded and sliced
2 leeks – sliced
½ jar (approx 90g) pesto
200g (7oz) goat's cheese
100g bag mixed salad leaves
4 tbsp ready-made French dressing
Oven: 200ºC, 400ºF, Gas Mark 6

Unroll pastry and cut into 8 squares. Put on a baking tray and cook in oven for 15 minutes. Meanwhile, heat the oil in a frying pan, add peppers and leeks and gently sauté for 15 minutes. Take pastry out of oven. Spread pesto on top of each square and top with peppers and leeks. Cut goat's cheese into cubes, including rind, and put on top.

※ May be made up to this point earlier in the day.

Put back in oven for 15 minutes. Serve with leaves and drizzle over dressing.

Cook's tip: Ready-rolled puff pastry can be bought from most large supermarkets and is sold refrigerated rather than frozen. All you have to do is unroll it, there is no need to roll it any thinner for this recipe. Alternatively, use 1½ blocks of puff pastry and rolled out to approximately ½cm (¼").

Opposite: Fe

QUICK CASSOULET WITH GARLIC BREAD

2 tbsp olive oil
1 onion – chopped
2 garlic cloves – crushed
200g (7oz) bacon – chopped
500g (1lb 2oz) Toulouse sausage – cut into thick slices
700g (1½lbs) fillet of pork or boned leg of lamb – fat removed and diced (ready diced meat can be obtained from some supermarkets)
2 tbsp flour
275ml (½pt) red wine
1 tin (400g) chopped tomatoes
2 handful of fresh chopped parsley
1 carton (284ml / ½pt) chicken stock – or use ½ stock cube and boiling water
2 tins (400g each) butter beans – drained
salt and pepper
2 loaves ready-made garlic bread or garlic bread slices

Cassoulet, which originates from Languedoc in Provence, consists of haricot beans cooked in a stew pot with pork rinds. Traditionally, it takes ages to prepare and cook as the beans have to be soaked overnight and then take several hours to cook. If you think pork rinds sound rather unappetising, don't worry, they are not used in this recipe and nor are the other fatty meats often used in cassoulets. This recipe can be prepared and cooked quickly by using tinned butter beans and a good cut of either pork or lamb.

Heat oil in a very large saucepan or flame-proof casserole. Add onion and garlic and gently fry for 3 minutes. Add bacon and sausage, cook for another 3 minutes, followed by lamb for a further 3 minutes. Stir in flour, then add red wine, tinned tomatoes, one handful of parsley and stock. Bring to the boil and allow to simmer gently for 40 minutes, stirring occasionally.
Add butter beans 10 minutes before the end of cooking and season (see Cook's tip below). If in a saucepan, transfer to an oven-proof casserole serving dish.

◗ May be made up to this point the day before.

If made in advance, re-heat cassoulet in oven: 190ºC, 375ºF, Gas Mark 5 with lid on for 45 minutes – 1 hour or until piping hot.

Cook garlic bread according to instructions on packet, separate pieces and place on top of cassoulet. Put back in oven, uncovered, for 10 minutes. Sprinkle with remaining chopped parsley and serve.

Cook's tip: Toulouse sausages are traditionally used in cassoulet but if you can't find them in the shops, use a spicy pork sausage instead. Taste before seasoning as the bacon and sausage make this dish quite salty.

BABY SPINACH LEAF SALAD WITH A RASPBERRY AND WALNUT VINAIGRETTE

400g baby spinach (can be bought in bags ready-washed)
DRESSING
8 tbsp walnut oil
2 tbsp raspberry vinegar
2 tsp French mustard
2 tsp honey
salt and pepper

The French generally keep their salads simple but go to town on the dressing. The walnut oil gives this dressing a deliciously nutty flavour and the raspberry vinegar and honey make it wonderfully sweet and fruity. You can make your own raspberry vinegar by adding raspberries to red wine vinegar and leaving them to infuse for a few days.

Mix all dressing ingredients together.

◗ Dressing may be made up to a week before using and kept in the fridge.

Put spinach leaves into a large salad bowl and toss in dressing.

Cook's tip: The easiest way to make the dressing is to put the ingredients into a jar and give it a good shake. The amount of dressing is quite generous so you may not need it all.

VACHERIN GLACÉ WITH SUMMER FRUITS AND CASSIS

500g (1lb 2oz) frozen summer fruits

250g (9oz) strawberries (optional) – hulled and cut in quarters

large slug cassis – approx 4 tbsp or more if you wish

1 litre good quality strawberry ice cream

8 ready-made meringues – (M & S ones recommended but other brands are also good)

Vacherin is a typically French dessert made of meringue with ice cream or whipped cream and sometimes fruit. You can make the meringue yourself, but as this book is all about taking short cuts, I suggest you buy them ready-made. Apart from fresh strawberries, all the other ingredients can be stored for a couple of months, making this an ideal dessert to "knock up" quickly if friends appear at the last minute.

Mix frozen summer fruit with strawberries and cassis and leave to de-frost. Transfer strawberry ice cream from tub into your own container (this will convince your guests that it is home-made!). Store in the freezer until ready to serve.

◖ May be prepared the day before.

To serve – put a meringue on each plate with a scoop of ice cream on top and spoon over fruit mixture.

Cook's tip: The best type of strawberry ice cream to buy is cream in colour and sometimes has pieces of strawberries in it. The usual pink variety looks and tastes rather artificial and "bought". If you can't find a really good strawberry ice cream, use vanilla instead.

M & S meringues look more "home-made" than most other brands. Some ready-made meringues look too white but as they are covered up by the ice cream and fruit it won't matter.

ORDER OF PREPARATION IF MAKING IN ADVANCE:

The day before:
1. Prepare cassoulet up to ◖
2. Make walnut and raspberry vinaigrette.
3. Mix summer fruits with cassis and strawberries. Transfer ice cream into bowl.

Earlier on the day:
4. Prepare pepper tarts.

In the evening:
5. Re-heat cassoulet and cook garlic bread.
6. Heat tarts.
7. Prepare spinach leaves and toss in dressing just before serving.
8. Assemble vacherin just before serving.

ORDER OF PREPARATION IN UNDER 2 HOURS:
1. Mix summer fruits with cassis and strawberries. Transfer ice cream into a bowl.
2. Prepare pepper tarts up to ☀ and heat as needed.
3. Make cassoulet.
4. Make walnut and raspberry vinaigrette and toss with spinach before serving.
5. Assemble vacherin just before serving.

PASSIONATE ABOUT GARLIC

Garlic lovers will adore these recipes. Not only do they taste scrumptious, but as garlic is claimed to have certain medicinal properties, think how healthy you will be after eating them. It is claimed that in the old days it was used to ward off evil spirits and safeguard against vampires. The only snag with garlic is that it sometimes wards off friends who haven't been eating it. There are two ways of helping to get rid of the smell on your breath. One is to chew fresh parsley and the other is to eat coffee beans. To make eating coffee beans more pleasant, you can buy chocolate coated ones which are delicious to serve with coffee after dinner.

ROCKET, PEAR AND WALNUT SALAD WITH A FROMAGE FRAIS DRESSING
MEDITERRANEAN SEAFOOD CASSEROLE WITH ROUILLE
FENNEL AU GRATIN
GARLIC AND PARSLEY BOILED POTATOES
BLACKCURRANT MARSHMALLOW RAMEKINS

♀ Californian Chardonnay. Recommendation – Sterling Winery Lake Chardonnay.

ROCKET, PEAR AND WALNUT SALAD WITH FROMAGE FRAIS DRESSING

There are said to be over 2000 varieties of pear in Europe. A few examples include Conference, Comice, Zépherine, Napolean and Wilhelminen. You can choose any type you like from the vast selection!

200g packet mixed salad leaves
40g (1½oz) rocket (or 2 plants)
100g (3½oz) walnut halves
4 ripe pears
juice of ½ lemon
8 tbsp ready-made "Fromage Frais Dressing" – Marks & Spencer recommended

Divide salad leaves and rocket between 8 individual plates and sprinkle walnuts on top. Peel and cut each pear into eight pieces, toss in lemon juice to prevent discolouring and arrange on top of salad. Drizzle with Fromage Frais Dressing. Serve with warm bread – see Handy Hints page 6.

Cook's tip: Instead of using fromage frais dressing, you can mix 2 tbsp fromage frais with 6 tbsp French dressing.

MEDITERRANEAN SEAFOOD CASSEROLE WITH ROUILLE

1 jar (approx 800ml) French Fish Soup – "Select Marée" recommended

1kg (2lbs 4oz) firm white fish, e.g. cod, halibut, plaice – filleted and skinned

500g (1lb 2oz) ready-to-eat mixed seafood – fresh or frozen and de-frosted

1 baguette

2 egg yolks

11 garlic cloves

8 heaped tbsp mayonnaise (approx 400 ml)

1 heaped tbsp tomato purée

This is a cross between a bouillabaisse and a main course variety of Corsican Fish Soup (page 28). It is wonderfully fishy and garlicky and always a great success.

Thinly slice baguette and brown under grill or in oven to make large croutons.

To make rouille – crush 3 cloves of garlic and mix with mayonnaise and tomato purée. Put half the rouille into a serving dish and mix the remainder together in a bowl with the egg yolks. Peel the remaining 8 cloves of garlic and put in a dish.

You should have three dishes to serve with the casserole: rouille, croutons and garlic cloves.

※ All the above may be prepared earlier in the day.

To make casserole – empty fish soup into a large saucepan and heat gently to boiling point. Cut white fish into chunks, add to soup and allow to simmer for 5 minutes. Add the mixed seafood and cook for a further 5 minutes. Take a small amount of soup and add to the bowl with the rouille / egg yolk mixture. Whisk together then put back into the saucepan and stir until the sauce thickens. Do not allow to boil or the eggs will curdle.

Serve casserole with croutons, garlic cloves and rouille. Guests should be told to take croutons, rub garlic over them and put rouille on top.

This recipe is not for people who dislike garlic.

Cook's tip: It is very important to use a good quality fish soup in this recipe. Shellfish soups may also be used, e.g. crab or lobster bisque.

FENNEL AU GRATIN

8 small heads of fennel or 6 large ones

8 tsp grated Parmesan

2 tbsp olive oil

salt and pepper

Oven: 200ºC, 400ºF, Gas Mark 6

Fennel looks a bit like short, fat, hairy celery. It has a unique aniseed flavour and is delicious baked with Parmesan.

Trim and wash fennel, reserve and chop the feathery leaves for decoration. Cut fennel heads into quarters and cook in salted boiling water for 10 minutes, or until tender. Drain and pack closely in an oven-proof serving dish in one layer. Sprinkle with Parmesan, season and drizzle over the olive oil.

※ May be prepared up to this point earlier in the day.

Put in oven for 25 minutes and sprinkle with reserved leaves before serving.

Cook's tip: If you have any fennel left over, it is delicious eaten cold, tossed in French dressing.

GARLIC AND PARSLEY BOILED POTATOES

1.5kg (3lbs 5oz) potatoes

570ml (1pt) milk

50g (2oz) butter or "Olivio"

2 garlic cloves – crushed

1 handful fresh chopped parsley

salt and pepper

The potatoes absorb the milk which they are boiled in, giving them a lovely creamy texture. This recipe may be varied by mashing the potatoes with any remaining milk and then sprinkling the parsley on top.

Scrub potatoes and cut into 2.5cm (1") cubes. Place in a saucepan with milk, butter or Olivio, crushed garlic, half the parsley and season. Bring to the boil and simmer uncovered for 20 minutes until tender. At this stage most of the milk will be absorbed but you may need to drain away any remaining milk. Put into a serving dish and sprinkle with remaining parsley.

Cook's tip: Keep some extra parsley to chew after the meal to get rid of the smell of garlic, if you're worried about it.

BLACKCURRANT MARSHMALLOW RAMEKINS

200g bag marshmallows

300ml (½pt) double cream

900g (2lbs) tinned blackcurrants (or other fruit may be used)

2 kiwi fruit – peeled and sliced into 8

1 packet "Tuiles Amandes" biscuits or other delicate biscuits

This is a wonderfully "gooey", sticky pudding. Your friends will spend hours trying to work out how you made it.

Put marshmallows in a microwave bowl, cover with cling-film, leaving a gap for steam to escape, and put in microwave on medium for 1½ minutes. Alternatively melt in a saucepan gradually over a very low heat. Whisk cream until stiff. Drain blackcurrants and fold into cream with the melted marshmallows. Put into 8 ramekin dishes and chill for at least 2 hours.

◗ ❄ May be made the day before or frozen.

Serve chilled in ramekins and decorate with slices of kiwi and "Tuiles Amandes".

Cook's tip: If you melt the marshmallows in a saucepan, watch them carefully as they are prone to burn.

ORDER OF PREPARATION IF MAKING IN ADVANCE:

The day before:
1. Make marshmallow ramekins.

Earlier on the day:
2. Prepare fish casserole up to ❄
3. Prepare fennel up to ❄

In the evening:
4. Make starter.
5. Cook potatoes.
6. Finish off cooking fennel and fish casserole.
7. Put bread in oven to warm.

ORDER OF PREPARATION IN UNDER 2 HOURS:
1. Make marshmallow ramekins.
2. Prepare fennel and put in oven as necessary.
3. Prepare fish casserole up to ❄ and finish as necessary.
4. Cook potatoes as needed.
5. Make starter and warm the bread.

"AND HERE'S ONE I MADE EARLIER"

You will probably find it difficult to believe that this complete menu can be prepared the day before. All you have to do prior to your dinner party is throw a few things in the oven. I can't reiterate enough how little you'll have to do on the night. The only problem is, you will be so relaxed that your friends will be convinced you got caterers in to do everything.

CRAB AND SPINACH MOUSSE
FRENCH POT ROAST CHICKEN WITH GARLIC KEBABS,
NEW POTATOES, TOMATOES, ONION AND ROSEMARY
BROCCOLI AU GRATIN
CHOCOLATE PECAN PIE

♀ A full flavoured white. Recommendation – Fairview Semillon from South Africa

6 tbsp dry white wine or water
1 sachet (11g) gelatine
2 small dressed crabs or 2 tins (170g) crab meat and 1 tin (43g) dressed crab
500g (1lb 2oz) frozen leaf spinach – de-frosted and drained
4 heaped tbsp mayonnaise
200g (7oz) cream cheese – the low fat type may be used
250g (9oz) prawns in shells
2 lemons – sliced
oil
salt and pepper

CRAB AND SPINACH MOUSSE

A crab has two sorts of meat. The white meat which is chewy and dense can be found in the claws and body. The brown meat which has a stronger flavour is found inside the hard upper shell. There are apparently over 4500 species of crab found world-wide – fortunately my local supermarket only sells one, so the choice isn't too mind boggling.

Brush a 23cm (9") ring mould or bowl with oil. Heat the wine or water to boiling point, sprinkle gelatine on top and stir until dissolved. Leave to cool. (See Handy Hints page 6 for tips on gelatine.) Put crab meat, spinach, mayonnaise, cream cheese, salt and pepper in a food processor to blend. Add cooled gelatine and pour into ring mould. Put in fridge for at least 2 hours.

◗ May be made up to this point the day before.

To serve – loosen edges of mousse with a palate knife and turn out onto a serving plate.

Decorate with lemon slices and prawns in shells. Serve with rolls or interesting bread.

Cook's tip: Fresh crabs give this mousse a far more intense flavour but they need to be eaten on the day of buying or the day after.

FRENCH POT ROAST CHICKEN WITH GARLIC KEBABS, NEW POTATOES, TOMATOES, ONION AND ROSEMARY

8 breasts of chicken with skin
1.5kg (3lbs 5oz) small new potatoes
8 tomatoes – cut into quarters
4 small onions – peeled and cut into quarters
few sprigs rosemary – chopped
3 tbsp olive oil
500g (1lb 2oz) passata
275ml (½ pt) dry white wine
salt and pepper
16 garlic cloves – peeled and thread on to 8 cocktail sticks – 2 cloves on each stick (you will probably need 2 bulbs)
Oven: 200ºC, 400ºF, Gas Mark 6

With this recipe, literally everything is thrown together into one pot (or rather two roasting tins). All the flavours infuse into each other while cooking and the garlic kebabs become tender and mellow as they roast.

You will probably need two roasting tins for these quantities. Divide all ingredients between roasting tins.

◗ May be prepared up to this point the day before.

Cook in oven for 1¾ hours, covered with foil for the first hour and then uncovered for the remainder, tossing occasionally. Half an hour before the end of cooking, make sure chicken and garlic kebabs are at the top of the roasting tins to brown.

Cook's tip: Chicken portions may be used instead of chicken breasts if you prefer.

BROCCOLI AU GRATIN

1.5kg (3lbs 5oz) broccoli – cut stalks off and separate into florets or you can buy the broccoli already in florets in which case you will only need 1kg (2lbs 4oz)
1 tub (300g-350g) ready-made Cheese sauce
110g (4oz) Cheddar – grated
Oven: 190ºC, 375ºF, Gas Mark 5

This is a variation of cauliflower cheese. I find cauliflower can be rather insipid in colour and this is why I have used broccoli for its vibrant green.

Put broccoli florets into boiling water and cook for approximately 6-8 minutes, but leave slightly crunchy. Drain well and put into an oven-proof serving dish. Put cheese sauce on top and sprinkle with grated Cheddar.

◗ May be prepared up to this point earlier in the day or the day before.

Put in oven for 30 minutes and serve.

Cook's tip: This recipe is also delicious using celeriac, peeled, cut into thick match sticks and boiled until crunchy but tender.

CHOCOLATE PECAN PIE

250g (9oz) ready-made short crust pastry
200g (7oz) dark chocolate
50g (2oz) butter
150ml (¼ pt) double cream
4 tbsp golden syrup
4 tbsp brown sugar
200g (7oz) pecans – buy them in packets already shelled
4 eggs
Oven: 180ºC, 350ºF, Gas Mark 4

It's a good job that this recipe serves a very generous 8 people. It is so wildly wicked that they will be coming back for more. A great Colorado-based dessert which makes a good back-up when guests arrive unexpectedly. Keep one in the freezer for such occasions.

Roll out pastry and line a tart tin (preferably loose-bottomed) approx 26cm (10½") in diameter. Prick the base with a fork and put in fridge while preparing the filling.

Melt chocolate, butter, cream, golden syrup and sugar in a saucepan over a gentle heat until dissolved (do not allow to boil). Beat in eggs and pecans. Pour into prepared pastry case and cook in oven for 1 hour.

◗ ✳ May be prepared the day before or may be frozen.

May be served hot or cold with fromage frais, crème fraîche or ice cream.

To re-heat – put back in oven for 15 minutes.

Cook's tip: For a variation of this recipe, you could use a mixture of nuts and raisins.

ORDER OF PREPARATION IF
MAKING IN ADVANCE:

The day before:
1. Make crab and spinach mousse.
2. Make chocolate pecan pie.
3. Prepare broccoli up to ◗
4. Prepare pot roast up to ◗

Earlier on the day:
5. Put your feet up, play tennis / golf, have a massage, go to work.

IN THE EVENING:
6. Turn on oven and put pot roast and broccoli in as necessary.
7. Turn out mousse.
8. Re-heat pecan pie while eating main course.

ORDER OF PREPARATION IN
UNDER 2 HOURS:
1. Make crab and spinach mousse.
2. Make pot roast and put in oven.
3. Make pecan pie.
4. Prepare broccoli and put in oven as needed.

EXTRAVAGANT AND MEGA-IMPRESSIVE

Y ou may need to re-mortgage your house, but this dinner party is sure to impress the boss, boyfriend, girlfriend, in-laws or anyone else.

♀ *A crisp aromatic white and a full bodied Pinot Noir. Recommendation – Villa Maria Private Bin Sauvignon Blanc from New Zealand and Cono Sur Reserve, Pinot Noir from Chile*

SMOKED SALMON TIMBALES
BOEUF EN CROÛTE
GRATIN OF POTATOES
PETIT POIS À LA FRANÇAISE
LAYERED ICED WHITE AND DARK CHOCOLATE TERRINE

SMOKED SALMON TIMBALES

An elegant starter which always makes guests feel special.

oil
400g (14oz) smoked salmon slices
250g (9oz) fromage frais
300g (11oz) taramasalata
2 lemons
black pepper
100g bag mixed salad leaves
6 tbsp ready-made French dressing (M & S Lite French Dressing recommended)

Brush the inside of 8 ramekin dishes with oil. Line with smoked salmon, reserving a couple of slices for lining the top. Mix together fromage frais, taramasalata, zest and juice of half a lemon and black pepper. Divide the mixture between the lined ramekins and seal with the remaining smoked salmon on top. Cover with cling-film and chill for at least 2 hours.

◗ May be made up to this point the day before.

To serve – gently run a knife round the edge of the ramekins and turn timbales out on to individual serving plates. Arrange leaves around the outside, drizzle with dressing and decorate with remaining 1½ lemons cut into wedges. Serve with warm rolls.

Cook's tip: You can now buy a wonderful selection of interesting rolls. Small, delicate ones with various toppings, e.g. poppy seeds, sesame seeds, go well with this starter. The part-baked ones would also go well.

BOEUF EN CROÛTE

This is something that most people never have the nerve to make. These are made individually with filo pastry and are easy to cook and serve successfully. Putting the boeuf en croûte straight onto a hot baking tray means that the bottom of it starts cooking immediately and helps to prevent the pastry go soggy.

10g (1¼oz) butter
olive oil
8 x 110g (4oz) fillet steaks
1 tub (110g) mushroom pâté
75g (3oz) mushrooms – chopped
1 packet or 24 sheets filo pastry (measuring approx 30cm x 18cm)
salt and pepper
Oven: 200ºC, 400ºF, Gas Mark 6

Melt butter and 1tbsp olive oil in a frying pan and when hot, put the steaks in, to brown the outside (approximately 20 seconds each side). Leave to cool.

Mix mushroom pâté with chopped mushrooms and season. Spread on top of each steak and wrap in filo pastry:– you will need 2½ sheets per steak. Lay out the first sheet and brush half lightly with oil. Fold in half and place steak on it diagonally, then fold corners into the centre to seal. Repeat the same process with the second sheet, turning the beef over so that the folded side is facing down and making sure that the oil is brushed between each layer. Brush top with oil. Cut another sheet of filo in half, crinkle up and place on top. Brush top again with oil.

☀ May be made up to this point earlier in the day.

Brush a baking tray with oil and put in oven for a few minutes to heat. Put boeuf en croûte on to hot tray and cook in oven for 20-25 minutes.

Cook's tip: You may think that crinkling up half a piece of filo is pretty stupid but it actually looks very effective and hides any mess underneath.

GRATIN OF POTATOES

Always popular and handy that it can be made in advance. It needs no last minute attention and as it is cooked in the dish in which it is served, you can take it straight from the oven to the table.

25g (1oz) butter or "Olivio"
300ml (½pt) double cream
300ml (½pt) milk
1 garlic clove – crushed
1.5kg (3lbs 5oz) potatoes – scrubbed
50g (2oz) grated Parmesan
salt and pepper
Oven: 180ºC, 350ºF, Gas Mark 4

Grease an oven-proof serving dish. Mix together cream, milk and crushed garlic. Thinly slice potatoes (may be done in a food processor). Layer potatoes in the dish with butter / "Olivio", salt, pepper and half the Parmesan dotted between the layers. Pour cream mixture on top, sprinkle with remaining Parmesan, cover with foil and cook for 1¾ hours. Take silver foil off for the last half hour for the top to brown.

◐ ☀ May be made up to this point the day before and frozen after cooking and cooling.

To re-heat – put in oven for 30 minutes.

Cook's tip: Easy alternative – buy 3 large packets of Marks & Spencer "Creamy Potato Gratin" and turn them into an oven-proof dish. Cook as instructions on packet.

PETIT POIS À LA FRANÇAISE

25g (1oz) butter or "Olivio"

2 medium onions – thinly sliced

225g (8oz) rindless bacon – chopped

6 large lettuce leaves (preferably cos) – shredded

284ml (½ pt) beef or chicken stock – can be bought in cartons or made with 1 stock cube and boiling water

900g (2lbs) frozen petit pois

Peas are one of the few vegetables which I prefer frozen because they are always tender and sweet. It may sound like an odd combination to put soggy lettuce with peas but it really goes well and is extremely popular with the French where the recipe originated.

Melt butter or "Olivio" in a large saucepan. Add onions and bacon and gently cook for 10 minutes until onion is soft. Stir in shredded lettuce.

✴ May be prepared up to this point earlier in the day.

Add stock to pan and bring to the boil. Add peas and simmer for 15 minutes, by which time the stock will have slightly reduced. Serve with remaining stock.

Cook's tip: The stock serves a double purpose, to cook the peas in and to add moisture when eating the boeuf en croûte.

LAYERED ICED WHITE AND DARK CHOCOLATE TERRINE

500ml (1pt) chocolate truffle ice cream (or the richest dark chocolate ice cream that you can find!)

100g (4oz) ratafia biscuits – crushed

250g (9oz) prunes (pitted and ready to eat) – chopped

4 tbsp brandy

150g (5oz) white chocolate

300ml (½pt) double cream

TO DECORATE (optional)

150ml (¼pt) single cream

1 bottle of chocolate sauce – "Smuckers" recommended

This recipe just can't fail to impress and is ideal for chocoholics. Not necessarily the best thing for a low calorie diet but you can console yourself by the fact that the prunes are good for you.

Line a 1.5 litre terrine or loaf tin with foil. Allow chocolate ice cream to slightly soften and push down evenly into the bottom of the tin. Mix the prunes with 2 tbsp of the brandy and spread on top of the ice cream. Put in the freezer while preparing the remaining ingredients.

Break the white chocolate up into cubes, put in a bowl and melt – either in microwave on medium for 3 minutes or until melted (see Handy Hints page 6), or put in a bowl over simmering water until melted. Add remaining 2 tbsp brandy to the cream and whisk until thick. Add melted chocolate and whisk in, then stir in crushed ratafia biscuits. Spread on top of terrine, cover and put back in freezer for at least 2 hours.

◗ ✴ May be made in advance and kept in the freezer until ready to serve.

To serve– turn out onto a serving plate, remove foil and slice. May be decorated on individual plates with 1 tbsp cream put to one side of the plate and 1 tbsp chocolate sauce on the other or put the cream and chocolate in jugs to hand round separately.

ORDER OF PREPARATION IF MAKING IN ADVANCE:

The day before:
1. Make chocolate terrine.
2. Make smoked salmon timbales.
3. Make potatoes au gratin up to ◗

Earlier on the day:
4. Prepare peas up to ✴
5. Prepare boeuf en croûte up to ✴

In the evening:
6. Turn out timbales and prepare for serving.

7. Re-heat potatoes and cook boeuf en croûte and peas as needed.

ORDER OF PREPARATION IN UNDER 2 HOURS:
1. Make terrine.
2. Make potatoes and put in oven.
3. Make smoked salmon timbales.
4. Brown steaks in a frying pan and leave to cool.
5. Prepare pea recipe and cook.
6. Make boeuf en croûte and put in oven when necessary.

MELLIFLUOUS MOMENTS

The meaning of mellifluous (Oxford Dictionary) is sweet-sounding. Synonyms of mellifluous (Collins Thesaurus) are rich, dulcet, bright, vivid, warm, intense, vibrant. Take a moment to think about this and I'm sure you will agree that this is the perfect name for this menu.

WARM DUCK AND MANGETOUT SALAD WITH A MARMALADE DRESSING
MUSSELS, SOLE AND ASPARAGUS IN A PUFF PASTRY CASE
NEW POTATOES WITH LEMON AND DILL
SUGAR SNAP PEAS AND BABY CORN
CHERRY, KIRSCH AND WHITE CHOCOLATE MOUSSE

*♀ New World Sauvignon Blanc.
Recommendation –
Errazuriz Sauvignon Blanc
from Chile*

WARM DUCK AND MANGETOUT SALAD WITH A MARMALADE DRESSING

The combination of duck, marmalade and soy sauce is quite delectable.

4 duck breasts
200g bag mixed salad leaves
4 tbsp sesame oil (olive oil may be used instead)
200g (7oz) mangetout – top and tail and cut in half on the diagonal
3 tbsp thick cut marmalade
3 tbsp soy sauce

Remove skin and fat from duck breasts and cut breasts into thin strips. Either put salad leaves in a large bowl or on 8 individual plates.

Heat 1 tbsp of the oil in a large frying pan and add duck. Fry for approximately 2 minutes until duck has browned. Add mangetout, marmalade and soy sauce. Allow to cook for a further minute. Finally add remaining 3 tbsp sesame oil. Put the duck and dressing on top of the leaves and serve immediately. Serve with warm bread or rolls – see Handy Hints page 5.

Cook's tip: This could also be served as a light lunch for 4.

MUSSEL, SOLE AND ASPARAGUS IN A PUFF PASTRY CASE

An exquisite dish of delicate fish and asparagus sandwiched between layers of light flaky pastry. You'll have problems believing it's so easy to make!

375g packet ready-rolled puff pastry
1 egg – beaten
500g (1lb 2oz) mussels – ready-cooked and shelled
1kg (2lbs 4oz) lemon or Dover sole – ask fishmonger to bone and skin them or other fish may be used, e.g. plaice, haddock, cod, salmon
1 tin "Campbell's" condensed cream of asparagus soup
200ml crème fraîche
2 glasses dry white wine
1 tin (approx. 400g) asparagus – drained
salt and pepper
Oven: 200°C, 400°F, Gas Mark 6

To make puff pastry cases – unroll pastry and cut into 8 squares. With a sharp knife mark the surface of the squares with a diamond pattern. Put onto a baking tray and brush with beaten egg.

✸ May be prepared up to this point earlier in the day and kept in a fridge.

Put puff pastry squares in oven for 20 minutes until golden and puffed up. Meanwhile, cut fish into slices or chunks and with all remaining ingredients, except asparagus, put in a large saucepan and allow to cook gently for 10 minutes. Add asparagus and continue cooking for a further 5 minutes.

Cut pastry squares in half horizontally, place bottom half on each serving plate, divide fish between them and put the top back on.

Cook's tip: If you prefer you can use fresh asparagus, but it will need to be cooked first in boiling water for approximately 6 minutes.

NEW POTATOES WITH LEMON AND DILL

These new potatoes absorb the wonderful flavours of the lemon, dill and olive oil.

1.5kg (3lbs 5oz) new potatoes

1 lemon – zest and juice of half

1 handful fresh chopped dill

2 tbsp olive oil

salt and pepper

Cook the potatoes in boiling, salted water until tender – about 20 minutes. Drain and toss in other ingredients.

Cook's tip: I find a zester works more efficiently than a grater to remove the lemon rind. A grater tends to take away some of the pith as well – not to mention the tips of your fingers.

SUGAR SNAP PEAS WITH BABY CORN

These two vegetables look attractive and, cooked quickly, give a real crunch.

500g (1lb 2oz) sugar snap peas – top and tail

300g (10oz) baby corn

Drop sugar snap peas and baby corn into boiling, salted water and cook for 5 minutes.

Drain and serve.

Cook's tip: These can both be cooked in the same pan together.

CHERRY, KIRSCH AND WHITE CHOCOLATE MOUSSE

Kirsch is a colourless brandy made from wild cherries and their stones. It tastes delicious with the chocolate and cherries in this mousse.

200g (7oz) white chocolate

300ml (½pt) double cream

1 jar (600g) cherry compote – "Bonne Maman" recommended

slug kirsch (approx 4 tbsp) – or other liqueur, e.g. brandy, Cointreau, Drambuie

To melt chocolate – break chocolate up into cubes, either put in a bowl and microwave on medium for 3-4 minutes until melted or put in a bowl over simmering water until melted. Meanwhile, whisk cream until thick. Fold in melted chocolate, cherry compote and kirsch. Put into 8 ramekin dishes and chill for at least 1½ hours.

❂ May be made the day before or may be frozen and serve chilled.

Cook's tip: If you buy a bottle of kirsch and wonder what to use it for, other than in this recipe, you can make a "Raffles Knockout Cocktail" – mix equal quantities of kirsch and Cointreau with a dash of fresh lemon juice – it's a knockout!

ORDER OF PREPARATION IF MAKING IN ADVANCE:

The day before:
1. Make cherry, kirsch and chocolate mousse.

Earlier on the day:
2. Prepare puff pastry to ❂

In the evening:
3. Prepare all ingredients for remaining recipes.

4. Cook potatoes and keep warm while eating starter.
5. Make starter.
6. Put puff pastry squares in oven while eating starter.
7. Put fish on to cook while eating starter.
8. Cook sugar snap peas and baby corn.

ORDER OF PREPARATION IN UNDER 2 HOUR' SAME ORDER AS ABOVE.

NO SPRING CHICKEN

Poussin is often known as spring chicken, but as this recipe is in the autumn section, I could think of no other name than "No Spring Chicken"! Having said that, as poussins are available all the year round, this menu is equally suitable to be served in spring or winter. It could be served in summer but as artichokes would not be available, you would need to eliminate them from the Potato and Artichoke Boulangère recipe or use a different potato recipe altogether.

♀ *Suggested Wine: South African Pinotage. Recommendation – Beyerskloof Pinotage*

BAKED RED PEPPERS WITH ANCHOVIES AND MOZZARELLA
POUSSIN VERONIQUE WITH ROAST BABY ONIONS
SPINACH BELLE VUE
POTATO AND ARTICHOKE BOULANGÈRE
RATAFIA ICE CREAM CAKE WITH A BUTTERSCOTCH SAUCE

BAKED RED PEPPERS WITH ANCHOVIES AND MOZZARELLA

4 large red peppers
2 tins anchovies in olive oil
8 spring onions – chopped
3 garlic cloves – chopped
250g (9oz) mozzarella
4 tomatoes – sliced
1 bunch watercress
Oven: 200ºC, 400ºF, Gas Mark 6

These baked peppers as so delicious that even people who swear they can't bear anchovies, will enjoy them cooked this way. They are equally good served hot or cold. I prefer to serve them cold as they can be cooked in advance and therefore give you one less thing to worry about at the last minute.

Cut red peppers in half, remove seeds and white membrane but leave green stalks on. Place on a baking tray, skin side down. Fill with anchovies, including oil, spring onions and garlic. Put in oven for 50 minutes.

Cut mozzarella into 8 slices and put inside peppers when they come out of the oven. May be served immediately, decorated as below, or left to cool and served cold.

◑ May be made up to this point the day before.

Serve decorated with tomato slices, watercress and warm crusty bread – see Handy Hints page 6.

Cook's tip: These peppers are also great for a casual lunch. Just double the quantities, to give each person two half peppers and serve with a salad and warm bread.

POUSSIN VERONIQUE WITH BABY ROAST ONIONS

4 poussins

500g (1lb 2oz) shallots

1 jar (500g) "Chicken Tonight – Country French Chicken Sauce"

200ml crème fraîche

275ml (½pt) dry Vermouth or white wine

200g (7oz) green, seedless grapes – cut in half

salt and pepper

Oven: 200ºC, 400ºF, Gas Mark 6

Poussins look attractive to serve for a dinner party. They may be messy, especially if you pick the bones up in your fingers, but are great fun to eat. I have allowed half a poussin per person, but if they are very small and your guests have large appetites, you can allow a whole poussin each. I find shallots are such a pain to peel, so in this recipe the soft skin is left on. They look and taste good cooked this way, but if you prefer, they can be peeled completely.

Cut each poussin in half and put in a roasting dish, skin side up. Top and tail shallots and remove outer skin only (may be peeled completely if preferred). Put shallots in the roasting dish with poussins.

Sieve "Chicken Tonight" sauce (discard the remaining bits) into a bowl and mix together with crème fraîche, Vermouth, grapes, salt and pepper. Pour sauce over poussins.

☀ May be prepared up to this point earlier in the day.

Cook in oven for 1 hour, basting occasionally. Serve poussins and shallots with the sauce.

Cook's tip: The same recipe may be used with chicken portions or breasts.

SPINACH BELLE VUE

2kg (4lbs 8oz) frozen leaf spinach

2 garlic cloves – crushed

1 tsp freshly grated nutmeg (optional)

1 small carton (150g) natural yoghurt

salt and pepper

I created this recipe while working in Verbier, Switzerland. When a guest asked me what it was called, I quickly had to think up a name. Looking out of the window at the beautiful view of mountains, I named it "Spinach Belle Vue" and the name has remained ever since.

Cook spinach from frozen as instructions on the packet. Drain well and add garlic, nutmeg and season well. Just before serving add yoghurt and make swirling patterns in the spinach.

Cook's tip: Fresh nutmeg is well worth the few seconds it takes to grate as it gives the spinach a sweet nutty flavour.

POTATO AND ARTICHOKE BOULANGÈRE

1kg (2lbs 4oz) potatoes – scrubbed

500g (1lb 2oz) Jerusalem artichokes – scrubbed

1 packet "Knorr" French Onion Soup

570ml (1pt) boiling water

Oven: 180ºC, 350ºF, Gas Mark 4

The Jerusalem artichokes give this potato dish a deliciously unusual taste. They tend to be rather knobbly, irregular in shape and difficult to peel. That is why neither the artichokes nor potatoes are peeled – why waste time when they taste just as good, if not better, with the skins on? Jerusalem artichokes are usually available from September to April but if you can't find them in the shops, either miss them out altogether and use extra potatoes, or grow you own.

Grease a large gratin dish. Thickly slice potatoes and artichokes to about 1cm

(½") thickness. Put in layers in gratin dish. Mix soup mix with boiling water and pour over potatoes and artichokes. Cover with foil and cook in oven for 1¾ hours. Uncover for the last half hour to allow the top to brown.

◗ May be made up to this point the day before.

To re-heat – put back in oven for 30 minutes.

Cook's tip: To save time, the potatoes and artichokes may be sliced in a food processor, but if you slice them thickly, it doesn't take too long and adds a certain chunkiness to the dish.

RATAFIA ICE CREAM CAKE WITH A BUTTERSCOTCH SAUCE

2 litres toffee or ice cream

200g (7oz) ratafia biscuits

large slug liqueur (approx. 4 tbsp) e.g. brandy, Baileys, Tia Maria

1 bottle butterscotch sauce – "Smuckers" recommended

This ice cream is made in a cake tin, but can also be done in a bowl and served as a "Bombe". It is so delicious it's sure to have your guests asking for second helpings.

Line a 23cm (9") cake tin with cling-film. Allow ice cream to soften slightly. Roughly crush half the ratafias and mix into the ice cream with the liqueur. Put into the prepared tin, arrange remaining ratafias on top and put in freezer for at least 2 hours. (If using a bowl, put ratafias on top once the "bombe" has been turned out of the bowl.) Keep in the freezer until ready to serve.

To serve – take ice cream out of cake tin, remove cling-film and put on a serving plate, biscuit side up. Put butterscotch sauce into a jug and serve with slices of ice cream cake.

Cook's tip: Other flavours of ice cream can be used, such as vanilla or white chocolate.

ORDER OF PREPARATION IF MAKING IN ADVANCE:
The day before:
1. Make ratafia ice cream cake.
2. Make potato and artichoke Boulangère.
3. Prepare baked peppers up to ◗

Earlier on the day:
4. Prepare poussins up to ☼

In the evening:
5. Cook poussins as needed.
6. Re-heat potatoes.
7. Make spinach belle vue.
8. Put baked peppers on plates and heat bread.

ORDER OF PREPARATION IN UNDER 2 HOURS:
1. Make ratafia ice cream cake.
2. Prepare and cook potato and artichoke Boulangère
3. Prepare poussins and cook as necessary.
4. Make baked pepper recipe and serve hot.
5. Make spinach belle vue.

A VEGETARIAN DINNER

With the ever-growing number of vegetarians, it's handy to have a couple of non-meat and fish menus up your sleeve. These days vegetarian food can be really exciting, not the boring old nut roast and lentils. I have chosen filo baskets as the main course as they can either contain a vegetarian filling or be filled with fish or meat for non-vegetarians.

MUSHROOM STROGANOFF
FILO BASKETS WITH BROCCOLI, LEEKS AND CHÈVRE
STUFFED BAKED PEPPERS WITH BULGUR WHEAT AND PESTO
ENDIVE AND WALNUT SALAD
APRICOT, YOGHURT AND MUESLI COMPOTE

♀ A New World Sauvignon. Recommendation – Lenswood Sauvignon Blanc from Australia

MUSHROOM STROGANOFF

You can't get much more mushroomy than this. I have used button mushrooms for this recipe as they can be left whole and stay firm.

750g (1lb 10oz) small button mushrooms
2 garlic cloves – crushed
2 tubs (300g–350g) fresh ready-made mushroom sauce
bunch spring onions – thinly sliced
2 handful fresh chopped parsley
slug dry or medium sherry (approx 4 tbsp)
salt and pepper

Wipe dirt off mushrooms and mix with remaining ingredients but reserve half the chopped parsley for decoration.

☼ May be made up to this point earlier in the day.

Microwave method – put in a large bowl and microwave on high for 8 minutes, stirring occasionally.
Conventional method – put in a saucepan and cook over a gentle heat, stirring occasionally, for 10 minutes or until piping hot.

Serve with remaining chopped parsley and warm crusty bread (see page 5)

Cook's tip: Mushrooms can be wiped with a damp cloth to remove dirt. If they are really filthy, they may need to be washed but drain them well as they are apt to retain water.

FILO BASKETS WITH BROCCOLI, LEEKS AND CHÈVRE

So many people are petrified about using filo pastry and as a result, your guests are always impressed. Don't be put off by this recipe before you have even started. Once you have got over your paranoia and made the first basket, the next seven will seem a cinch. You'll wonder why you went into terminal depression in the first place!

1 packet fresh filo pastry – or 16 sheets (measuring approx 30cm x 18cm)
olive oil
1kg (2lbs 4oz) leeks – sliced
500g (1lb 2oz) broccoli florets
200ml crème fraîche
1 tub (300g-350g) fresh ready-made cheese sauce
500g (1lb 2oz) log or 4 individual rounds of chèvre
salt and pepper
Oven: 180ºC, 350ºF, Gas Mark 4

To make filo baskets – you will need oven-proof bowls to mould the filo in (about 11cm/ 4" in diameter). Brush the inside of the bowls with oil. Lay one sheet of filo out and brush half of it with oil and fold it in half to form a square. Brush top of square with oil and repeat with another sheet of filo on top – you should now have 4 layers of filo. Place filo in bowl and brush exposed pastry with oil. Repeat for each bowl. Cook in oven for 10 minutes. When cool enough to handle, take out of the bowls and you are left with the filo baskets.

Put the sliced leeks and broccoli florets into boiling water and cook for 3-4 minutes until al dente.

☼ May be prepared up to this point earlier in the day.

◗ ❅ The filo baskets may be made the day before or frozen.

Mix together broccoli, leeks, crème fraîche, cheese sauce, salt and pepper and put into baskets. Slice chèvre into 8 thin rounds and put on top. Put back in oven for 20 minutes.

Cook's tips: Fresh filo is more pliable and easier to handle than the frozen variety. It is also handy to freeze if you have any left over. If you can only get frozen filo and you find it is very brittle, don't worry. The baskets are far tougher than you think. As there are four layers of filo to each basket, make sure any torn places are in the middle and that the one on the outside is intact. You will probably find that the packet of filo will contain more sheets than you need so you should have some spare if any get ruined. For non-vegetarians you could fill the baskets with salmon in dill hollandaise – see recipe on page 17.

ENDIVE AND WALNUT SALAD WITH A WALNUT DRESSING

400g bags ready prepared endive (may contain other leaves as well) or 2 heads curly endive
100g (3½oz) walnut pieces
DRESSING
8 tbsp walnut oil
2 tbsp balsamic vinegar
1 tsp French mustard
salt and pepper

A simple salad with a wonderful, flavourful dressing.

If necessary, wash the endive, dry well and break up into a large salad bowl. Reserve a handful of walnuts (approx. 20g) and add the rest to the endive. To make dressing – put the handful of walnuts into a food processor or liquidizer with the dressing ingredients to blend. Pour dressing over the salad, toss and serve.

◗ The dressing may be made in advance and will keep in the fridge in an air-tight jar for 2 weeks.

Cook's tip: If you are in a real rush, put the walnut pieces in with the endive and use a ready-made dressing.

STUFFED BAKED PEPPERS WITH BULGUR WHEAT AND PESTO

4 large red peppers
300g (11oz) bulgur wheat
1 jar (170g) pesto
1 tin (400g) chopped tomatoes
1 handful fresh basil for decoration (optional)
salt and pepper
Oven: 190ºC, 375ºF, Gas Mark 5

Two of my favourite ingredients are bulgur wheat and red peppers so what could be more perfect than stuffing one inside the other. The bulgur wheat has a wonderful crunchy, nutty texture and goes well with the smooth sweetness of the peppers.

Soak bulgur wheat in plenty of cold water for about half an hour. Cut peppers in half, remove the seeds and white membrane but leave the stalks on. Drain bulgur wheat and mix with pesto and chopped tomatoes, including the juice.

Season well. Stuff inside peppers, put in a baking dish and cover with foil.

☼ May be prepared up to this point earlier in the day.

Cook in oven for 50 minutes. Decorate with whole basil leaves and serve.

Cook's tip: These peppers can also be served cold but will need some French dressing poured over them to keep them moist.

APRICOT, YOGHURT AND MUESLI COMPOTE

1 jar (600g) apricot compote –
"Bonne Maman" recommended

12 tbsp muesli, "Jordan's Crunchy
Crisp", "Nut Feast" or similar
crunchy breakfast cereal

250ml (9fl oz) carton ready-made
custard (fresh or long-life)

250g (9oz) Greek yoghurt

A lovely light dessert which takes minutes to make. The cereal gives it a surprising crunch.

You will need 8 ramekin dishes or 8 glasses to serve these in. Put apricot compote at the bottom, followed by 1 tbsp muesli or other cereal. Mix custard with Greek yoghurt and put on top. Put in fridge to cool for at least 1 hour.

❋ May be made the day before or frozen.

Sprinkle a further teaspoon of cereal over the top before serving chilled.

Cook's tip: Other fruit compotes may be used, e.g. cherry, gooseberry, etc. If you have any left over, you can eat it for breakfast.

ORDER OF PREPARATION IF
MAKING IN ADVANCE:

The day before:
1. Make apricot compote up to ❋
2. Make filo baskets.
3. Make dressing for salad.

Earlier on the day:
4. Make mushroom stroganoff up to ❋
5. Cook leeks and broccoli for filo baskets.
5. Make stuffed peppers up to ❋

In the evening:
6. Fill filo baskets and cook when needed.
7. Make salad and dress just before serving.

8. Heat mushroom stroganoff as needed.
9. Put stuffed peppers in oven when needed.
10. Sprinkle cereal on top of compote before serving.

ORDER OF PREPARATION IN
UNDER 2 HOURS:
1. Make apricot compote.
2. Prepare stuffed peppers and put in oven as needed.
3. Make filo baskets and prepare filling.
4. Make salad and dress before serving.
5. Make mushroom stroganoff.

A WAIST WATCHER'S DINNER

Low fat dinner parties don't have to be boring – look at this one. If you know that your guests coming to dinner have just joined "Weight Watchers" or are on low cholesterol diets, why not try and help so that they can really enjoy themselves and don't feel deprived.

SPINACH SOUP WITH BACON CROUTONS AND BAKED GARLIC BREAD
CHICKEN, MUSHROOM AND LEEK PARCELS WITH CORIANDER RICE
MANGETOUT AND GINGER STIR-FRY
FRUIT CRUDITÉS WITH A FRUITY FROMAGE FRAIS DIP

*♀ New World Chardonnay.
Recommendation – Casablanca*

SPINACH SOUP WITH BACON CROUTONS

A lovely thick warming soup. The bacon croutons are actually bacon flavoured soya chips, available from most large supermarkets. They taste just like bacon but contain a fraction of the fat content and all you have to do is sprinkle them out of the packet.

900g (2lbs) frozen chopped spinach

850ml (1½pts) chicken stock (made with 2 stock cubes or cartons of ready-made stock)

1 large potato – diced

2 large onions – chopped

1 tsp nutmeg (preferably freshly grated)

275ml (½pt) milk

1 small pot (150g) natural yoghurt

50g (2oz) bacon flavoured soya bits

salt and pepper

Put frozen spinach, stock, diced potato, chopped onions, nutmeg, salt and pepper into a large saucepan. Bring to the boil and then allow to simmer for 20 minutes or until the potato is soft. Blend in a liquidizer or food processor until smooth.

◗ ❋ May be made up to this point the day before or may be cooled and frozen.

To re-heat – add milk and heat gently until piping hot. Pour into soup bowls and decorate with a swirl of yoghurt and scatter bacon bits on top.

Cook's tip: There is no need to peel the potato, just give it a scrub before dicing it.

BAKED GARLIC BREAD

2 heads of garlic

1 ciabatta or French loaf

Oven: 190°C, 375°F, Gas Mark 5

This is a healthy way to eat garlic bread. It tastes just as good and is great fun to eat. Baking garlic in this way turns it into a purée and gives it a milder, more mellow flavour.

Remove papery outer covering of garlic heads but do not separate or peel the cloves. Wrap the garlic heads in foil and bake for 1 hour.
Meanwhile, sprinkle bread with water, wrap in foil and put in oven for 10 minutes.

To serve – slice bread, and separate garlic cloves. Each guest should squeeze the garlic out of the clove and spread the purée on the bread.

Cook's tip: Squeezing garlic out of a clove is similar to squeezing toothpaste out of a tube but at least you don't have to put the top on afterwards.

CHICKEN, MUSHROOM AND LEEK PARCELS WITH CORIANDER RICE

8 chicken breasts – skinned and boned

150g (5oz) mushrooms – sliced

2 large leeks – sliced

1 handful fresh chopped coriander

2 packets "Bachelor's Coriander and Herb Rice"

2 tins "Campbell's Condensed Consommè"

large slug dry sherry (approx. 4 tbsp)

salt and pepper

Oven: 190ºC, 375ºF, Gas Mark 5

Everything is cooked together in a foil parcel which seals in all the flavours. Each guest should be given a parcel to unwrap themselves, making this dish incredibly easy to serve.

Cook rice according to instructions on packet (if making in advance allow rice to cool).

☀ May be prepared up to this point earlier in the day.

Lay out 8 pieces of foil with the sides pulled up and divide the rice between them. Place a chicken breast on top followed by the mushrooms, leeks and coriander. Season and pour 2 tbsp of consommé over each one. Wrap up in the foil, seal well.

Put on an oven tray and cook for 40 minutes.

Put the remaining consommé and the sherry into a saucepan and allow to simmer for 15 minutes. Pour into a sauce boat and serve with the chicken.

Cooks tip: The foil parcels should resemble Cornish pasties and be well sealed to keep in all the juices and flavours.

MANGETOUT AND GINGER STIR-FRY

1kg (2lbs 4oz) mangetout – topped and tailed

2 garlic cloves – crushed or chopped

2.5cm (1") cube fresh root ginger – chopped

3 tbsp soy sauce

No oil is used in this stir-fry.

Heat the soy sauce, garlic and ginger in a wok or large frying pan until sizzling. Add the mangetout and cook rapidly for 3-5 minutes.

Cook's tip: This tastes so much better and crisper when it is freshly cooked. I suggest you prepare all the ingredients and cook it after you have finished the soup. As the chicken parcels take no last minute preparation and the stir-fry only takes a few minutes, this won't be too difficult and will ensure that it is crisp when served. It can be served in the wok, assuming your wok isn't too old and battered to take to the table.

FRUIT CRUDITÉS WITH A FRUITY FROMAGE FRAIS DIP

Choose 4 of the different types of fruit:

500g (1lb 2oz) strawberries
500g (1lb 2oz) raspberries
4 bananas – sliced
100g (3½oz) physalis (cape gooseberries)
350g (12oz) fresh lychees
4 kiwi – peeled and cut in quarters
4 pears – peeled and sliced
Anything else you like the look of
8 small pots (100g each) low fat fruit flavoured fromage frais ("Shape" or other brand)

A light, fresh, easy dessert which looks pretty.

Put fromage frais into 8 ramekin dishes. Place on individual plates with fruit arranged around them.

Cook's tip: If you are using pears or bananas squeeze lemon over them to stop browning.

ORDER OF PREPARATION IF
MAKING IN ADVANCE:

The day before:
1. Make soup, cool and put in fridge overnight.

Earlier on the day:
2. Cook rice and allow to cool.
3. Top and tail mangetout.
4. Put fromage frais dip into ramekin dishes, cover with cling-film and refrigerate.

In the evening:
5. Prepare chicken parcels and cook as needed.
6. Prepare fruit for crudités.

7. Put soy sauce, garlic and ginger in a wok and stir-fry mangetout just before serving.
8. Prepare baked garlic bread and put in oven when necessary.
9. Re-heat soup.

ORDER OF PREPARATION IN
UNDER 2 HOURS:
1. Cook rice.
2. Make soup and prepare baked garlic bread. Cook as needed.
3. Prepare mangetout stir-fry and cook as needed.
4. Assemble chicken parcels and put in oven as necessary.
5. Prepare fruit crudités and dip.

Winter

WINTER FRUIT PLATTER

Choose three of the following fruit and arrange on a large platter.

CAPE GOOSEBERRIES (physalis)
DATES (fresh)
GRAPES (black or white) – cut into little bunches of 8-10
KUMQUATS, LYCHEES
Nuts in shells look pretty to serve with fruit
PINEAPPLE – peeled, sliced, halved and core removed
STAR FRUIT – sliced
TANGARINES

COOKING IN ADVANCE

This menu is ideal for busy people as virtually everything can be prepared the day before, enabling you to work all day, and have time for a relaxing bath (and a gin and tonic) before even having to think about cooking.

♀ A smooth full bodied red. Recommendation – Havenscourt Roti from California

SALAD OF CHICKEN LIVER PÂTÉ ON CROSTINI WITH
RED ONION MARMALADE
NUTTY, HERBED STUFFED LAMB
CARROT AND CARDAMOM PURÉE
RÖSTI POTATO CAKES
TARTE AU CITRON

Opposite: Castle Townsend Banquet (page 130)

SALAD OF CHICKEN LIVER PÂTÉ ON CROSTINI AND RED ONION MARMALADE

1 tbsp olive oil

2 medium red onions – sliced

5 tbsp marmalade

1 long baguette (thin French loaf)

170g (6oz) ready-made chicken liver pâté (Marks & Spencer's recommended)

100g (3½oz) lamb's lettuce (corn salad)

Red onions are milder and sweeter than the brown skinned ones and they tend to keep their red-purple colour after cooking. The combination of the red onion marmalade and chicken liver pâté is quite delectable and makes this a really interesting salad.

To make the red onion marmalade – heat the oil in a saucepan. Add sliced onions and cook gently over a low heat with the lid on for 10 minutes. Add marmalade and continue to cook for a further 5 minutes, stirring occasionally. Cool, cover and keep refrigerated.

To make crostini – cut 24 slices from the baguette (approx 1 cm thick) and put under grill to turn golden. Cool and store in an air-tight container until needed.

◗ May be prepared up to this point a day or two before.

To serve – spread the pâté on to the crostini. Arrange the lamb's lettuce on 8 plates and put 3 crostini on top of the lamb's lettuce. Finally put 3 blobs (teaspoons) of red onion marmalade between the crostini. The red onion marmalade can be served warm or cold.

Cook's tip: You only need a small amount of chicken liver pâté so it's not worth making it yourself. The M & S one is excellent but there are many other very good ones around.

NUTTY, HERBED STUFFED LAMB

1 large leg lamb – with bone taken out to form a hollow in the middle (ask butcher or supermarket to do it for you)

3 garlic cloves

1 small onion – cut in quarters

1 handful fresh rosemary

1 handful fresh thyme

250g (9oz) ready soaked dried apricots

50g (2oz) pine nuts

275ml (½pt) red wine

275ml (½pt) orange juice

100ml crème fraîche

salt and pepper

Oven: 180°C, 350°F, Gas Mark 4

Not only is this recipe easy to make and cook but also to serve as it can be carved straight through without having to worry about any bones. The juices which the lamb is cooked in will have crème fraîche stirred into it and served as a sauce.

Trim fat off the lamb. Put 2 garlic cloves, onion and half the herbs in a food processor to chop, then add apricots and season. Stir in pine nuts. Push stuffing into lamb cavity and tie up with string to form the shape of a ball. Thinly slice remaining clove of garlic, make small slits in the lamb and push garlic in. Put remaining sprigs of herbs on top.

◗ ✳ May be prepared up to this point the day before or may be frozen.

Put in a roasting tin with wine and orange juice. Cook for 20-25 minutes per lb (450g) plus an extra 20 minutes. (Timing should be worked out by weight of lamb before boning – average cooking time 2-2½ hours.) Baste occasionally. Before serving, stir crème fraîche into juices in the tin. Carve lamb thickly and serve with juices.

Cook's tips: Use any red wine for this – it's not worth using anything too expensive. Trim off as much fat as possible from the lamb so that it won't make the sauce greasy.

Opposite: Mellifluous Moments (page 109)

CARROT AND CARDAMOM PURÉE

2kg (4lbs 8oz) carrots

2 tsp cardamom pods

2 garlic cloves

25g (1oz) butter or "Olivio"

1 handful fresh chopped parsley

salt and pepper

The cardamom gives this carrot purée a lovely scented flavour. A lot of recipes tell you to split open the cardamom pod and just use the seeds. I always use the cardamom pod whole, because I find it too time consuming to de-seed and it gives the purée more flavour.

Peel and slice carrots. Boil for about 20 minutes until tender. Put cardamom in a food processor with the garlic to crush. Add drained carrots, butter or Olivio, salt and pepper and blend until smooth. May be served immediately with chopped parsley sprinkled on top or left to cool and refrigerated overnight.

◗ ❋ May be made the day before and may be frozen.

To re-heat – either microwave on high for 7 minutes stirring half way through, or cover with foil and put in oven: 190ºC, 375ºF, Gas Mark 5 for 20 minutes. Sprinkle chopped parsley on top.

Cook's tips: If you find it a real pain to peel so many carrots, frozen ones can be used instead. If you have any purée left over, add stock and turn it into a wonderful soup.

RÖSTI POTATO CAKES

2 packets long-life "Rösti" – (approx 400g each)

oil – to brush inside 8 ramekin dishes

Oven: 200ºC, 400ºF, Gas Mark 6

If you have tried to make rösti from scratch, it was probably the first and last time you ever made it. It's a real pain and this is why the packets of ready-made Rösti are so useful but there is no reason why your guests shouldn't think you spent hours making it.

Divide Rösti between the 8 oiled ramekin dishes.

◗ May be prepared the day before. Cover ramekins with cling-film and keep refrigerated – they won't discolour.

Remove cling-film and cook in oven for 40 minutes. Serve in ramekins.

Cook's tip: These packets are always handy to keep in your cupboard for emergencies.

TARTE AU CITRON

250g (9oz) ready-made short
crust pastry

3 lemons

4 eggs

225g (8oz) castor sugar

300ml (½pt) double cream

1 tbsp icing sugar

Oven: 170ºC, 325ºF, Gas Mark 3

A lovely tart tarte! There are many ready-made varieties but they all look "bought" and don't taste anything like as good as this one.

Roll out pastry and line a flan dish (preferably loose-bottomed) 25cm-26cm in diameter. Prick base with a fork and bake in oven for 15 minutes.

Put the zest and juice from the lemons, eggs and sugar in a food processor or liquidizer for 2 minutes. Add cream and blend for a further 30 seconds. Pour into prepared pastry case and cook for 45 minutes until set. Either serve immediately with icing sugar sieved on top, or leave to cool and store in fridge overnight.

◗ ❄ May be made the day before and may be frozen.

To re-heat – put in oven for 15 minutes and dust with icing sugar. May be served with fromage frais or crème fraîche.

Cook's tip: I never bother to use dried beans when baking pastry blind, if bubbles appear, just push them down with the back of a spoon.

ORDER OF PREPARATION IF
MAKING IN ADVANCE:

The day before:
1. Make crostini and red onion marmalade.
2. Prepare lamb up to ❄
3. Prepare carrot purée up to ❄
4. Prepare rösti up to ◗
5. Make tarte up to ❄

In the evening:
6. Cook or re-heat as needed.
7. Finish off chicken liver pâté salad.

ORDER OF PREPARATION IN
UNDER 2 HOURS:
1. Prepare lamb and cook as necessary.
2. Make carrot and cardamom purée.
3. Make crostini and red onion marmalade.
4. Prepare rösti and put in oven when needed.
5. Make tarte and cook while eating main course.
6. Finish off preparing salad.

A BLACK, WHITE AND GOLD PARTY

I once arranged a birthday party for my husband with a black, white and gold theme and it was so popular that I have decided to include the recipes in this book. Not only is the food black, white and gold, but all your guests must dress in these colours. They are easy colours to dress in, unlike a green party I once held, as most people have something with these colours in their wardrobe. If you like, you can make it a black tie party. Try and decorate the room in black, white and gold – the possibilities are endless. If you wish, you can finish the meal with some black and white cheese (there is a cheddar you can buy with a black rind) and instead of butter, use "Gold".

♀ *New World Fizz.*
Recommendation – Lindauer Brut N.V. from New Zealand (this has a black and gold label)
♀ *A ripe easy going white and red. Recommendations – Penfolds, Rawson's Retreat Bin 21 Semillon Chardonnay and Penfolds Bin 35 Shiraz Cabernet from Australia*

BLACK AND GOLD TORTILLA CHIPS WITH BLACK AND WHITE DIPS
SMOKED SALMON AND CREAM CHEESE WITH CAVIAR CHESS BOARD
CHICKEN WITH WILD MUSHROOMS AND BLACKEYE BEANS
BLACK AND WHITE RICE
CRUNCHY CABBAGE AND CARAWAY SALAD
WHITE CHOCOLATE ROULADE WITH A DARK CHOCOLATE SAUCE
BLACK, WHITE AND GOLD FRUIT PLATTER

BLACK AND GOLD TORTILLA CHIPS WITH BLACK AND WHITE DIPS

150g (5oz) fromage frais or Greek yoghurt
5 heaped tsp black olive paste
1 tub onion and garlic dip or any other white dip
1 large packet tortilla chips
1 large packet "Blue Corn" tortilla chips

Tortilla chips evolved from triangles of corn tortillas that were grilled or fried to crisp them up. I have used the regular ones which are a gold colour and "blue corn" which are actually black!

Mix fromage frais or yoghurt with black olive paste and put into a small serving bowl. Also put onion and garlic dip into a bowl. Place bowls on platters and arrange tortilla chips around them.

Cook's tip: You could also serve an aubergine dip – available in tubs from Waitrose – which is a blackish colour.

SMOKED SALMON AND CREAM CHEESE WITH CAVIAR CHESS BOARD

8 slices pumpernickel bread

4 slices smoked salmon
(approx 110g /4oz)

½ lemon

100g (3½oz) cream cheese

1 small jar black lumpfish caviar

If goldfish are called goldfish, then smoked salmon can be described as gold! This is a bit of poetic license but it looks very effective and tastes good.

Put a slice of smoked salmon on four of the pieces of pumpernickel and cut into quarters. Squeeze lemon juice over them. Spread remaining four slices of pumpernickel with cream cheese and cut into quarters. Put a small blob of caviar on top. Arrange on a platter like a chess board.

Cook's tip: These are ideal to have with drinks.

CHICKEN WITH WILD MUSHROOMS AND BLACKEYE BEANS

1 packet "Knorr Mushroom and Garlic Soup" or other brand mushroom soup

275ml (½pt) boiling water

8 chicken breasts – skinless and boneless – cut into strips

2 tins (400g) blackeye beans – drained

2 garlic cloves – crushed

1 glass dry Vermouth or white wine

200g (7oz) wild mushrooms, e.g. morilles, porcini, shiitake, oyster – washed and sliced or cut in half

200ml crème fraîche

salt and pepper

Oven: 190°C, 375°F, Gas Mark 5

Blackeye beans are creamy in colour with a "black eye" which is where they were joined to the pod. They are an ideal ingredient for a black, white and gold party.

Put soup into a large oven-proof casserole dish and mix with boiling water. Add all other ingredients, except the mushrooms and crème fraîche. Cover casserole and cook for 1½ hours, adding the mushrooms and crème fraîche 15 minutes before the end of cooking. If making in advance, do not add mushrooms and crème fraîche until re-heating.

◗ ❋ May be made the day before or may be frozen once completely cooled.

To re-heat – put back in oven for 45 minutes – 1 hour until piping hot. Add mushrooms and crème fraîche 15 minutes before the end of cooking.

Cook's tips: Buy the blackest wild mushroom you can find to give this dish a good black and white effect. If you can't find blackeye beans, use cannellini beans instead.

BLACK AND WHITE RICE

450g long-grain and wild rice

You can now buy packets of ready mixed white and wild rice.

Cook rice as instruction on packet.

CRUNCHY CABBAGE AND CARAWAY SALAD

1 medium-sized white cabbage

250g (9oz) baby corn – cut in half

2 large handfuls (100g) currants or raisins

1 small pot (150ml) yoghurt

2 tsp caraway seeds

4 tbsp ready-made French dressing

The caraway seeds and cabbage go so well together in this lovely fresh, crunchy salad.

Cut cabbage in quarters and remove the hard core. Coarsely shred, put in a large salad bowl and mix with all remaining ingredients.

Cook's tip: Cumin seeds can be used instead of caraway seeds for change.

WHITE CHOCOLATE ROULADE WITH A DARK CHOCOLATE SAUCE

200g (7oz) white chocolate

5 eggs

6 level tbsp castor sugar

300ml (½pt) double cream

1 bottle chocolate sauce "Smuckers" recommended

Oven: 180°C, 350°F, Gas Mark 4

Roulades are always popular. This one is made extra special and unusual by using white chocolate.

Grease a Swiss roll tin and line with baking parchment. Break the chocolate up into cubes, put in a bowl and melt – either microwave on medium for 3-4 minutes (see Handy Hints page 6), or put bowl over simmering water until melted. Separate the eggs and whisk the whites until stiff. Add the sugar to the yolks and whisk until pale. Whisk the melted chocolate into the yolk and sugar mixture. Fold in egg whites and pour into prepared tin. Cook for 15 minutes. Leave to cool, put another piece of baking parchment on top and cover with a damp tea towel. Whisk cream until stiff.

◖ ✳ May be prepared up to this point the day before but the roulade must be kept covered with a damp tea towel or may be frozen.

Turn roulade out of tin on to the baking parchment. Spread with cream and roll up, using the baking parchment to help. Put the chocolate sauce into a serving jug, slice the roulade and serve.

Cook's tips: The reason for whisking the egg whites first, is that you don't have to wash up the whisk before whisking the yolks. Once the white chocolate has melted, it needs to be immediately whisked into the yolks otherwise it will harden quickly. If it begins to harden, don't panic, just keep whisking and it won't matter if there is an odd lump.

BLACK, WHITE AND GOLD FRUIT PLATTER

1 honeydew melon – skin and pips removed and cut into slices

1 bunch black grapes – cut into small bunches of around 8

250g (9oz) cape gooseberries (physalis)

Arrange on a large platter.

ORDER OF PREPARATION IF
MAKING IN ADVANCE:

The day before:
1. Make chicken recipe.
2. Make roulade up to ✳

In the evening:
3. Prepare tortilla chips and dips.
4. Prepare chess board.
5. Make salad.
6. Re-heat chicken.
7. Cook rice.
8. Roll up roulade.
9. Make fruit platter.

ORDER OF PREPARATION IN
UNDER 2 HOURS:
1. Make roulade, allow to cool and roll up.
2. Prepare chicken and cook as necessary.
3. Prepare tortilla chips and dips.
4. Prepare chess board.
5. Cook rice as needed.
6. Make salad.
7. Prepare fruit platter.

COCKTAIL CANAPÉS

You would think that making a few nibbles for a drinks party would be quick and easy but canapés can be incredibly time consuming. The following are recipes which can be made effortlessly and, in some cases, in advance. Here are a few golden rules when making canapés. Keep it simple, limit the number of different types of canapé to six. As a general guide, allow 6 pieces per person per hour. Arrange the food on large platters and constantly replenish to fill gaps. With this kind of finger food, there is no need to provide plates but make sure you have plenty of paper napkins to pass around.

Suggested Sparkling Wine: New World Fizz. Recommendation – Angas Brut from Australia

GRUYÈRE AND SMOKED SALMON ROULADES
MALAYSIAN CHICKEN KEBABS WITH SATAY SAUCE
CROUSTADES WITH GARLIC PRAWNS
AVOCADO AND MANGO DIP WITH GRISSINI AND VEGETABLE CRUDITÉS
MINI SAUSAGES WITH A MARMALADE GLAZE
FRESH FRUIT KEBABS
Serves 16 – 20

ALTERNATIVE RECIPES FOR COCKTAIL PARTIES
Black and White Tortilla Chips with Black and White Dips – page 124
Bruschetta with Feta and Sun–dried Tomatoes – page 58
Crostini with Mozzarella, Black Olives and Anchovies – page 19
Croustades with Egg Mousse and Mock Caviar – page 52
Dips with Cheese Straws and Bagel Chips – page 135
Marinated Olives and Feta – page 52
Mini Tartlettes of Mushroom, Bacon and Brie – page 61
Smoked Salmon and Cream Cheese with Caviar Chess Board – page 125
Smoked Salmon Dip with Pitta Triangles – page 144
Tapas – page 79
Mini Tartlettes of Leeks, Bacon and Cambozola – page 91
Tomato and Goat's Cheese Puffs – page 55

GRUYÈRE AND SMOKED SALMON ROULADES

These delicate roulades are half the size of a normal one and look very elegant to serve for a drinks party. This quantity will make 2 roulades which should be thinly sliced.

4 eggs
175g (6oz) gruyère – grated
150ml (¼pt) double cream
1 tub (approx 230g) smoked salmon pâté (can also use smoked trout pâté or Boursin)
bunch watercress
1 lemon
salt and pepper
baking parchment
Oven: 190ºC, 375ºF, Gas Mark 5

Grease a Swiss roll tin (or two if you have them) and line with baking parchment. Separate eggs and mix yolks with grated gruyère, cream, salt and pepper. Whisk egg whites until stiff and fold into cheese mixture.

Pour half the roulade mixture into the prepared tin (or tins) and cook for 12 minutes. Turn onto a sheet of foil and leave to cool. Repeat the same process with the other half the mixture if you have not already done so.

Spread the smoked salmon pâté over the roulades, roll up, using the foil to help.

◑ May be prepared up to this point the day before, wrapped in the foil and kept in the fridge.

To serve – slice thinly and arrange on a platter with watercress and slices of lemon.

MALAYSIAN CHICKEN KEBABS WITH A SATAY SAUCE

8 skinless chicken breasts

2 red peppers

2 green peppers

1 jar satay marinade – "Sharwoods" recommended

1 jar satay sauce – "Sharwoods" recommended

48 cocktail sticks

Oven: 190ºC, 375ºF, Gas Mark 5

These mini chicken kebabs look very colourful interspersed with the red and green peppers. Satay sauce is like a spicy peanut dip which tastes sensational with the chicken. The quantity below will make 48 kebabs but can easily be adapted for larger numbers of guests.

Cut chicken breasts into ½" cubes. De-seed peppers and cut into chunks. Thread 2-3 pieces of chicken on to each cocktail stick, interspersed with a chunk of red and green pepper. Put into an oven-proof dish and pour over satay marinade. Cover and marinate for at least 1 hour or preferably overnight in a fridge.

◗ May be made up to this point the day before.

Cook kebabs uncovered in oven for 25 minutes. Heat satay sauce according to instructions.

To serve – put on a large platter with the sauce in a bowl in the middle and the kebabs arranged around it.

Cook's tip: An alternative to satay chicken is pesto chicken. Substitute the satay marinade for pesto and mix 4 heaped tbsp mayonnaise with 1 tbsp pesto for the dip.

CROUSTADES WITH GARLIC PRAWNS

24 slices brown bread (thin or medium sliced)

olive oil

400g (14oz) prawns – fresh or frozen and de-frosted

6 heaped tbsp mayonnaise

2 garlic cloves – crushed

paprika

Oven: 190ºC, 375ºF, Gas Mark 5

Lovely crisp tarts made out of bread filled with deliciously garlicky prawns – makes 48.

Roll slices of bread with a rolling pin to flatten. With a small round pastry cutter, cut out two rounds out of each slice of bread. Push the 48 rounds into tart tins and brush with olive oil (this will probably have to be done in batches).

Put in oven for 10-15 minutes until golden. Allow to cool.
Mix prawns with mayonnaise and crushed garlic.

◗ May be made up to this point the day before and the croustades may be kept in an air-tight container for up to 2 days.

Divide mixture between croustades and sprinkle paprika on top. Keep in fridge until ready to serve.

May be prepared 2-3 hours before serving.

Cook's tip: Instead of making the bread croustades, you could buy ready-made mini pastry cases and fill them with the prawn mixture.

AVOCADO AND MANGO DIP WITH GRISSINI AND VEGETABLE CRUDITÉS

1 packet grissini (bread sticks)

1 cauliflower – cut into small florets

250g (9oz) sugar snap peas – topped and tailed

250g (9oz) cherry tomatoes

2 yellow peppers – de-seeded and sliced

DIP

2 ripe avocados

4 level tbsp (approx 120g) mango chutney

few drops chilli sauce (optional)

juice of ½ lemon

salt and pepper

The presentation of this is very important as it can either look sensational or pretty ordinary. I think dips and crudités always look good when presented on a large wicker platter or flattish basket. Arrange the vegetables in alternating colour groups and keep replenishing them when they run out.

Mash avocado with a fork and mix with remaining dip ingredients. Put into small serving bowls.

☼ May be prepared up to this point earlier in the day.

Place dip on large platters or wicker baskets and arrange grissini and crudités around them.

MINI SAUSAGES WITH A MARMALADE GLAZE

80 mini cocktail sausages – approx 1.2kg (2lbs 10oz)

4 heaped tbsp marmalade

Oven: 200ºC, 400ºF, Gas Mark 6

The amount of cooking time will depend on whether the sausages are in one layer or piled up on top of each other. When they are piled up, you may need to allow more time for cooking – there's nothing worse than a rare sausage!

Prick sausages with a fork, put in a roasting dish and toss in marmalade. Cook uncovered in oven for 1 hour or more basting with marmalade occasionally. Drain off fat and serve with cocktail sticks.

FRESH FRUIT KEBABS

Choose a selection of 4 of the following fruit:

Strawberries / Mango / Papaya / Black Seedless Grapes / Pineapple / Kiwi / Melon / Dried Apricots or Other Dried Fruit

48 cocktail sticks

Most people don't think of serving something sweet, but this provides a lovely refreshing ending to a cocktail party.

Prepare fruit and cut into "mouth-size" pieces. Thread onto cocktail sticks.

ORDER OF PREPARATION IF MAKING IN ADVANCE:

The day before:
1. Make roulades.
2. Prepare chicken kebabs and marinate.
3. Make croustades with garlic prawns up to ◑

Earlier on the day:
Make avocado and mango dip.

Or:
Thread on to kebab sticks,

cover with cling-film and keep cool until needed.
6. Fill croustades with garlic prawns.
7. Put avocado dip on platters with vegetable crudités.
8. Slice roulade and decorate.
9. Put mini sausages and marmalade into a roasting dish and put in oven as required.
10. Cook chicken satay and heat as needed.

ORDER OF PREPARATION IN UNDER 2 HOURS:
1. Prepare chicken kebabs,

marinate and cook as needed.
2. Make roulades and slice before serving.
3. Make croustades with garlic prawns.
4. Prepare sausages and cook as necessary.
5. Make avocado and mango dip and arrange on platters with vegetable crudités.
6. Make fruit kebabs.

CASTLE TOWNSEND BANQUET

In the South of County Cork, Ireland, lies a sleepy little village called Castle Townsend. I have spent many holidays lazing in peaceful tranquillity and enjoying some of the best wild salmon and duck I have ever eaten. The village is dominated by the 14th century castle and this menu conjures up images of a magnificent banquet, eaten in the grand dining room of the castle.

WARM SALMON AND WATERCRESS TIMBALES WITH HOLLANDAISE SAUCE
DUCK BREASTS WITH GLAZED ONIONS AND KUMQUATS
PARSNIP AND APPLE PURÉE
LEMON ROAST POTATOES
CHOCOLATE AND FRUIT FONDUE

Y A lightly oaked Chardonnay and a ripe fruity red. Recommendations – Montana, Marlborough Chardonnay from New Zealand and Franciscan Oakville Zinfandel from California

WARM SALMON AND WATERCRESS TIMBALES WITH HOLLANDAISE SAUCE

Even though I am happy to sit by the river with a fishing rod, I live in hope that I don't catch anything. I would personally far rather buy my salmon ready gutted, scaled, skinned and filleted! A timbale is a plain round, high-sided mould and the preparation cooked in it. If you don't have timbale moulds, there is no need to rush out and buy them, as ramekin dishes work just as well.

oil
700g (1½lbs) fresh salmon fillet – skinned
1 bunch watercress – approx. 75g
250ml crème fraîche – the low fat type may be used
2 eggs
salt and pepper
2 lemons – cut into 8 wedges
1 jar (250ml) hollandaise sauce
Oven: 190ºC, 375ºF, Gas Mark 5

Brush 8 timbale or ramekin dishes with oil. Put the salmon, half the watercress, crème fraîche, eggs and seasoning into a food processor until smooth. Put into the oiled timbales or ramekin dishes and cook in oven for 15-20 minutes until firm.

◐ ❄ May be made up to this point the day before or may be frozen.

To serve – turn salmon out of timbales or ramekins (you may need to run a knife round the edge to loosen them). If made in advance, put back in oven to re-heat for approximately 15 minutes.

Hollandaise sauce – either put in microwave on low for 2 minutes or stand in a bowl of very hot water for 5 minutes. Serve timbales with a wedge of lemon, sprig of watercress and warm hollandaise sauce. Warm bread or rolls may be served with the timbales.

Cook's tip: I suggest you put the hollandaise sauce in a small bowl to heat and destroy the jar it came in.

DUCK BREASTS WITH GLAZED ONIONS AND KUMQUATS

8 duck breasts

4 tbsp soy sauce

4 tbsp marmalade

16 kumquats – cut in half

4 large onions – peeled and cut in quarters

275ml (½ pt) orange juice

1 tsp ground ginger

salt

Oven: 220ºC, 425ºF, Gas Mark 7

When in Ireland during the shooting season, you may want to join a shoot and spend hours plucking ducks. Personally, I find it easier to buy duck breasts straight from the butcher or supermarket – it saves time. The cooking time for this recipe depends on whether you like your duck slightly pink, or better cooked.

Prick the skin of the duck with a fork and rub salt into it. Place, skin side up, on a rack over a roasting tin. Cook for 30-40 minutes. Mix 2 tbsp soy sauce and 2 tbsp marmalade together and use to baste duck 15 minutes before the end.

To make the sauce – put the remaining soy sauce and marmalade into a saucepan with kumquats, onions, orange juice and ginger. Bring to the boil and simmer for 30 minutes.

☼ The sauce may be made in advance and re-heated.

To serve – thinly slice duck breasts and fan out on individual plates. Pour the sauce over.

Cook's tip: Kumquats are sometimes quite pippy. Don't worry too much about removing all the pips. By the time the sauce has been simmering for 30 minutes, they are not particularly noticeable. The duck breasts look very impressive sliced and fanned out, but if you find this too much to do at the last minute, just leave them whole and pour the sauce on top.

PARSNIP AND APPLE PURÉE

8 parsnips – approx. 1kg (2lbs 4oz)

4 eating apples or 500g (1lb 2oz) apple purée

2 tsp curry powder

1 tsp brown sugar

salt and pepper

I think that apple and duck make perfect partners, so this purée is ideal to serve with the main course. It needs no last minute attention and can be made in advance and re-heated.

Peel and slice the parsnips and apples. Put into boiling water and cook for 20 minutes or until soft. (If using apple purée, cook parsnips separately and add purée later.) Drain parsnips and put in a food processor with remaining ingredients and purée until smooth.

◗ ❋ This dish may be made in advance or frozen and re-heated.

To re-heat – either microwave on high for 7 minutes, stirring half way though or put in an oven-proof serving dish, cover with foil in oven: 190ºC, 375ºF, Gas Mark 5 for 20 minutes.

Cook's tip: If you have frozen the purée, allow plenty of time for it to de-frost before re-heating.

LEMON ROAST POTATOES

1.5kg (3lbs 5oz) potatoes – scrubbed but not peeled
3 tbsp olive oil
zest and juice of 2 lemons
1 handful fresh chopped thyme
2 garlic cloves – crushed
salt and pepper
Oven: 200ºC, 400ºF, Gas Mark 6

You can't have an Irish banquet without potatoes! The addition of lemon and thyme and garlic makes these roast potatoes very special.

Cut potatoes into cubes – approximately 1cm (½"). Put in a roasting tin with remaining ingredients and toss. Cook for 1½ hours, tossing occasionally.

Cook's tip: Once you have prepared this, it must be put in the oven immediately otherwise the potatoes will turn brown. The potatoes will come to no harm if they are left in a bit too long in the oven – just turn the oven down a bit to stop them burning.

CHOCOLATE AND FRUIT FONDUE

1 bottle "Smucker's Chocolate Fudge Topping" (or other brand chocolate sauce)
Choice of 4 different types of fruit, e.g.:-
4 bananas – sliced
500g (1lb 2oz) strawberries
110g (4oz) physalis (cape gooseberries)
500g (1lb 2oz) raspberries
1 packet (500g) ready-soaked dried apricots
1 packet (500g) dried pears or 4 fresh pears – peeled and sliced

I have a friend from Belgium who came to a demonstration of this menu and was horrified to see me use a bottle of chocolate sauce. She told me that she would do this recipe but adapt it to use the real thing (melted chocolate from Belgium of course). I bumped into her a few days later in a local supermarket and guess what was in her trolley? Yes you're quite right – a bottle of chocolate sauce. This is so simple that you'll be looking for ways to complicate the recipe. Once you have served it and accepted all the compliments, you'll be making it over and over again.

Heat chocolate sauce – first tip contents of sauce into a bowl and put in a microwave for 2 minutes or follow instructions on bottle.

To serve – put chocolate sauce into 2 small serving bowls and place on 2 platters with fruit arranged round them. Give each person a fork or fondue stick to dip fruit into chocolate sauce.

Cook's tip: It is handy to keep a bottle of chocolate sauce and some dried apricots or pears in your store cupboard. If anyone drops round unexpectedly, you can "knock this up" in seconds using dried fruit and whatever fresh fruit you happen to have.

ORDER OF PREPARATION IF
MAKING IN ADVANCE:

The day before:
1. Make salmon timbales up to ❋
2. Make parsnip and apple purée up to ❋

Earlier on the day:
3. Make sauce for duck.

In the evening:
4. Prepare fruit for fondue (except for bananas which should be sliced just before serving). Turn chocolate sauce out into a bowl.
5. Cook potatoes as necessary.
6. Prepare duck and put in oven when necessary.
7. Re-heat parsnip and apple purée.
8. Finish off salmon timbales.

ORDER OF PREPARATION IN
UNDER 2 HOURS:
1. Prepare salmon timbales up to ❋ and heat as needed.
2. Prepare and cook potatoes as needed.
3. Make parsnip and apple purée.
4. Prepare duck and sauce and cook as necessary.
5. Prepare fondue.

THE NORMANS GO NORTH

Starting off with a French theme of Camembert, pork and Camargue rice, the menu then moves North using parsnips and eventually ends up in Scotland with Scotch Pancakes and a Whisky Mac Sauce – very international!

CAMEMBERT AND BLACKCURRANT FILO PARCELS
ROULADE OF PORK WITH PISTACHIO NUTS AND SUN-DRIED TOMATOES
RED CAMARGUE RICE
PARMESAN PARSNIPS
SCOTCH PANCAKES WITH PEAR, GINGER AND A WHISKY MAC SAUCE

*A ripe fruity red.
Recommendation – James Herrick,
Cuvée Simone. Vin de Pays d'Oc
from France*

CAMEMBERT AND BLACKCURRANT FILO PARCELS

These filo parcels are oozing with sumptuously sweet, gooey Camembert.

*1 packet filo pastry – or 12 sheets
(measuring approx 30cm x 18cm)*

olive oil

*1½ Camembert round cheeses – cut
into 8 triangles (in fact you will have
9 so you can eat one as you cook!)*

8 tsp blackcurrant jam

100g bag mixed salad leaves

8 tbsp ready-made French dressing

Oven: 190°C, 375°F, Gas Mark 5

Grease a baking tray. Cut sheets of filo in half so that you have 24 squares. Start by taking 3 squares and lightly brush each one with oil and lay on top of each other. Put a Camembert triangle in the centre and a teaspoon of blackcurrant jam on top. Draw up the pastry to seal up the filling, pinch together and brush with oil. Put on the baking tray and repeat the same process to make the remaining parcels.

◗ May be made up to this point the day before and kept uncovered in a fridge.

Put in oven for 15 minutes. Arrange salad leaves around the outside of 8 plates, pour dressing over and put Camembert parcel in middle.

Cook's tip: Keep checking the parcels as the tops are prone to burn.

ROULADE OF PORK WITH PISTACHIO NUTS AND SUN-DRIED TOMATOES

Pistachio nuts originated in the Middle East but the French often use them in terrines. They are also quite delicious cooked in this way.

*2 – 3 pork tenderloin fillets –
approx 1kg (2lbs 4oz)*

*1 jar (285g) sun-dried tomatoes in
oil – half will be used for this recipe
and half with the rice, the oil can
be used for the Parmesan parsnips*

*100g (3½oz) pistachio nuts –
ready-shelled*

1 tub (350g) fresh Napoletana sauce

*1 jar (475g) pasta sauce – "Ragu"
or "Dolmio" recommended*

salt and pepper

Oven: 190°C, 375°F, Gas Mark 5

Trim any fat off pork tenderloins and slit lengthways but do not cut right through. Cover with a piece of cling-film and beat with a rolling pin to flatten. Use half the sun-dried tomatoes and shake off the oil. Lay them down the middle of the pork with the pistachio nuts and season. Roll the pork up tightly and place in an oven-proof dish with the folds at the bottom – there is no need to secure them with string or cocktail sticks. Pour Napoletana and pasta sauces on top.

☼ May be prepared up to this point earlier in the day.

Cook in oven for 1 hour, basting occasionally. To serve – slice the pork and fan out on to plates. Pour sauce on top.

Cook's tip: If you can't find fresh Napoletana sauce, use 2 jars pasta sauce instead.

in oven for 1 hour, covered with foil for the first 30 minutes and uncovered for the remainder. Put stuffing balls in the oven for 40 minutes, uncovered. Put sauce into a saucepan and heat gently until piping hot. Drain any fat from the juices in the turkey pan and add to the sauce. Carve turkey breasts and serve with stuffing balls and sauce.

Cook's tip: The stuffing balls will become crisp and taste better if cooked separately but if you are short of space in the oven, they can be added to the roasting dish and cooked with the turkey.

PURÉE OF SWEET POTATO

1.5kg (3lbs 5oz) sweet potatoes

2 garlic cloves – crushed

50g (2oz) butter or "Olivio"

1 handful fresh chopped parsley

salt and pepper

Sweet potatoes have always been popular in America and are slowly becoming better known in England. This recipe is ideal for entertaining as it can be made in advance and even frozen.

Peel sweet potatoes, cut into chunks and put immediately into a saucepan of water to stop discolouring. Add a pinch of salt. Bring water to the boil and simmer for 20 minutes or until potatoes are very soft. Drain, return to the pan and add garlic, butter or "Olivio", half the parsley and season. Mash with a potato masher until smooth. Put into a serving dish and sprinkle remaining parsley on top.

◐ ✳ May be made the day before or frozen.

To re-heat – either microwave on high for 7 minutes, stirring half way through or put in an oven-proof serving dish, cover with foil and put in oven: 190°C, 375°F, Gas Mark 5 for 20 minutes.

Cook's tip: The flesh of sweet potatoes can either be orange or pale yellow in colour. The orange ones are better as they don't discolour so easily. The only way to tell which colour they are is to scratch away a little piece of the skin, but if you do this in the shop, make sure no one is looking!

GLAZED ROAST PARSNIPS
AND CARROTS

700g (1½lbs) parsnips

700g (1½lbs) carrots

4 tbsp olive oil

1 tbsp brown sugar

salt and pepper

Oven: 200°C, 400°F, Gas Mark 6

These two vegetables go well together to make an interesting and colourful dish.

Top and tail the parsnips and carrots and scrub clean. Cut into even-sized, chip-shaped wedges.

Put in a roasting tin with olive oil, brown sugar, salt and pepper and put in oven for 1 hour, tossing occasionally.

Cook's tip: There is no need to peel the parsnips and carrots which saves a bit of time.

Opposite: A "Classy" Brunch (page 144)

PUMPKIN AND WALNUT PIE

225g ready-made short-crust pastry

1 tin (454g) pumpkin

1 tin (400g) condensed milk

100g (3½oz) walnut pieces – chopped

2 tbsp brown sugar

1 heaped tsp ginger

1 heaped tsp cinnamon

3 eggs

Oven: 180°C, 350°F, Gas Mark 4

You can't have Thanksgiving without pumpkin pie. I think it can be rather bland, so I have added walnuts, to give it a bit of bite, and condensed milk to really liven it up.

Roll out pastry and line a tart tin or flan dish (preferably loose-bottomed) 25cm-26cm (10") in diameter. Mix all remaining ingredients together and put into prepared tart. Cook in oven for 1 hour.

◖ ❄ May be made in advance and frozen.

To re-heat – put in oven for 15 minutes.

Serve with cream, or ice cream – rum and raisin ice cream goes exceptionally well.

Cook's tip: When rolling pastry, always use plenty of flour and turn the pastry frequently as you roll it. Drape it over the rolling pin to lift it up when you turn it and lift it into the tart tin.

ORDER OF PREPARATION IF
MAKING IN ADVANCE:

The day before:
1. Make stuffing balls and sauce.
2. Make sweet potato purée.
3. Make pumpkin and walnut pie.

In the evening or morning if you are going to eat at lunch time:
4. Prepare parsnips and carrots and cook when needed.
5. Put turkey in oven and add stuffing balls as necessary.
6. Turn dips into your own bowls. Put cheese straws in oven as needed.
7. Re-heat sweet potato purée.
8. Heat sauce.
9. Re-heat pumpkin pie.

ORDER OF PREPARATION IN
UNDER 2 HOURS:
1. Make pumpkin and walnut pie.
2. Prepare parsnips and carrots and cook as necessary.
3. Prepare stuffing balls, sauce and turkey. Cook as necessary.
4. Make sweet potato purée.
5. Prepare dips, etc.
6. Re-heat pumkin pie if necessary.

Opposite: Free and Easy Boxing Day (page 141)

SHORT OF THYME

If you are short of thyme, you will have to find another herb to add to the pork; apart from that, this menu is ideal for you. Lovely warming recipes for entertaining in the winter.

FRENCH ONION SOUP WITH CHEESY CROUTONS
FILLET OF PORK WITH WILD MUSHROOMS AND THYME
SUN-DRIED TOMATO RICE
SPICY SPINACH AND RED ONION
NUTTY FUDGE TART WITH VANILLA ICE CREAM

♀ Southern French red. Recommendation – Chateau de Lascaux, Coteaux de Languedoc

1 loaf ciabatta – cut into 16 thin slices
2 garlic cloves
2 onions – thinly sliced
1 tbsp olive oil
4 cans (approx 400g each) good quality "French Onion Soup" – Baxter's recommended
5 tbsp brandy
225g (8oz) Gruyère cheese – grated
pepper
Oven: 190ºC, 375ºF, Gas Mark 5

FRENCH ONION SOUP WITH CHEESY CROUTONS

A lovely warm comforting soup which is always popular.

To make croutons – put slices of ciabatta on a baking tray and put in oven for 20 minutes, turning half way through, until golden. This can also be done under the grill. Rub both sides with garlic.

Heat oil in a large saucepan and quickly fry onions over a high heat until brown. Add cans of soup, brandy and pepper.

☼ May be prepared up to this point earlier in the day. The toasted ciabatta may be stored in an air-tight container for a couple of days.

Gently heat soup until piping hot. Put ¾ of the grated cheese on top of the croutons and put back in the oven for 10 minutes or under grill for a few minutes until cheese is bubbling. Ladle soup into bowls, put two croutons on top of each one and sprinkle with remaining cheese.

Cook's tip: French bread may be used instead of ciabatta.

1.2 kg (2½lbs) pork fillet
3 tsp French mustard
1 handful fresh chopped thyme or 2 tsp dried thyme
4 tbsp port or medium sherry
450g (1lb) mushrooms – preferably wild – choose a mixture, e.g. shiitake, oyster, chestnut, porcini, chanterelles
2 tbsp olive oil
1 tub (300g–350g) fresh mushroom sauce
200ml crème fraîche
salt and pepper

FILLET OF PORK WITH WILD MUSHROOMS AND THYME

You need thyme but not time for this recipe. A good selection of wild mushrooms give it a very special flavour.

Cut pork into thin slices or strips and mix with mustard, thyme, port or sherry, salt and pepper. Leave to marinate for 1 hour or longer (may be left over-night).

Wipe the mushrooms and slice or cut in half. Heat oil in a wok or large frying pan. Add pork with marinade and fry for approximately 7 minutes. Add mushrooms, fry for a further 5 minutes then add mushroom sauce and crème fraîche and continue to cook for a further 5 minutes.

☼ This is better cooked fresh but if you prefer, you can prepare it earlier in the day but do not add the crème fraîche until 5 minutes before the end of re-heating.

To re-heat – put in an oven-proof serving dish and cover with lid or foil. Put in oven: 190ºC, 375ºF, Gas Mark 5 for 45 minutes – 1 hour or until piping hot.

Cook's tip: Wild mushrooms are normally full of grit and dirt so it is important to wash them thoroughly.

SUN–DRIED TOMATO RICE

It takes about 17lbs of fresh tomatoes to make 1lb of the sun–dried produce. This is why their flavour is so concentrated. They transform the rice into a lovely red colour with an intense tomato flavour.

450g (1lb) long-grain rice
½ jar (approx 100g) sun-dried tomato paste
1.2 lt (2pts) vegetable stock (made with 2 vegetable stock cubes and boiling water)

Put rice in a saucepan and mix together with sun-dried tomato paste. Pour hot stock on top, bring up to the boil, stir and then allow to simmer for 20 minutes until all the liquid has been absorbed.

Microwave method – mix rice with sun-dried tomato paste in a microwave bowl and pour over hot stock. Cover with cling-film, leaving a gap for steam to escape, and microwave on high for 18 minutes. Stir half way through cooking.

Cook's tip: Rice cooked in this way can also be served cold as part of a rice salad.

SPICY SPINACH AND RED ONION

I find it a great disappointment to buy loads of fresh spinach, wash, de-stalk and cook it, only to find that you have a little pile in the bottom of the pan. That is exactly why I am using frozen spinach for this recipe. With the addition of all the other ingredients, I think you'll agree it tastes great.

1 tbsp olive oil
2 red onions – sliced
1 garlic clove – crushed
2 small red chillies – de-seeded and finely chopped or a few drops chilli sauce
2 tsp cumin seeds
1.5kg (3lbs 5oz) frozen leaf spinach – defrosted and drained
salt and pepper

Heat the oil in a large saucepan. Fry the onions until beginning to soften then add garlic and chillies and continue to fry for a further 2 minutes to brown. Turn heat down and add cumin, spinach and season generously. Gently cook for 10 minutes until heated through.

☼ May be made earlier in the day.

To re-heat – put in microwave on high for 7 minutes, stirring half way through.

Cook's tip: Take great care when chopping the chillies and wash your hands immediately afterwards to stop the heat transferring to anything else.

NUTTY FUDGE TART WITH VANILLA ICE CREAM

250g (9oz) ready-made short crust pastry

100g (3½oz) walnut halves

100g (3½oz) pecan halves

1 tin (405g) condensed milk

3 eggs

1 litre tub good quality vanilla ice cream

Oven: 190ºC, 375ºF, Gas Mark 5

Deliciously "gungy".

Allow ice cream to slightly soften and transfer to a serving bowl and return to freezer until ready to serve.

Roll out pastry and line a tart tin or flan dish (preferably loose-bottomed) 25cm-26cm (10") in diameter. Prick base with a fork and bake in oven for 10 minutes. If bubbles appear, just push them down again.

Put nuts in the cooked pastry case. Beat eggs, mix with condensed milk and pour over nuts. Cook in oven for 30 minutes. Serve with ice cream.

❍ ❄ May be made in advance or may be frozen.

To re-heat – put in oven for 15 minutes.

Cook's tip: This can also be served with cream, crème fraîche or yoghurt.

ORDER OF PREPARATION IF MAKING IN ADVANCE:

The day before:
1. Make nutty fudge tart and transfer ice cream.

Earlier in the day:
2. Prepare soup up to ❄
3. Prepare pork up to ❄
4. Prepare spinach up to ❄

In the evening:
5. Heat soup and finish off cheesy croutons.
6. Re-heat pork, and spinach.
7. Cook rice.
8. Re-heat tart.

ORDER OF PREPARATION IN UNDER 2 HOURS:
1. Marinate pork.
2. Transfer ice cream, prepare tart and cook when necessary.
3. Prepare soup and croutons and heat when needed.
4. Cook rice and spinach as necessary.
5. Cook pork.

FREE AND EASY BOXING DAY

If you want to actually enjoy Christmas and not spend most of your time slaving over a hot stove, this is a wonderful menu which will enable you to spend as little time as possible in the kitchen. All the following recipes can be made in advance and frozen. So you can enjoy Christmas day, eat, drink, be merry and all you have to remember is to take the dishes out of the freezer.

♀ A spicy, fruity Syrah / Shiraz. Recommendation – McDowells Syrah from California

FETA AND CRANBERRY TARTS ON A BED OF ENDIVE
CASSEROLE OF PHEASANT WITH ORANGE AND CHESTNUT
TOASTED SESAME DUCHESSE POTATOES
HARICOTS VERTS WITH SAUTÉED ONIONS
CHRISTMAS TIRAMISU

FETA AND CRANBERRY TARTS ON A BED OF ENDIVE

These little tarts with the red berries on top and green leaves of the endive look very pretty and festive.

175g (6oz) feta cheese
1 packet "Rahms" 24 mini croustades (or other mini pastry shells)
1 jar (195g) cranberry sauce
8 tbsp olive oil
2 tbsp balsamic vinegar
120g bag of endive or 1 whole endive
salt and pepper
Oven: 190ºC, 375ºF, Gas Mark 5

Cut or crumble feta into small cubes and put into pastry shells. Put a blob of cranberry sauce on top.

❄ May be frozen at this stage but allow to defrost completely before heating.

To make dressing –put olive oil, balsamic vinegar, 3 teaspoons cranberry sauce, salt and pepper into a jar and shake well until mixed together.

Put tarts in the oven for 15 minutes and arrange on a bed of endive with dressing drizzled on top.

Cook's tip: These can either be served as a starter at the table or the tarts can be put on a platter and passed round with drinks.

CASSEROLE OF PHEASANT WITH ORANGE AND CHESTNUTS

8 boneless breasts of pheasant
500g (1lb 2oz) shallots – peeled
4 heaped tbsp thick cut marmalade
1 tin game soup – "Baxters Royal Game Soup" recommended
275ml (½pt) red wine
275ml (½pt) orange juice
450g (1lb) frozen or tinned chestnuts
1 handful fresh chopped parsley
salt and pepper
Oven: 190°C, 375°F, Gas Mark 5

I have been put off cooking pheasant in the past because it can so often be tough. However breasts are always tender and are now available from supermarkets and some butchers.

Cut pheasant breasts into chunks and put in a large casserole dish with all ingredients except the chestnuts and parsley. Cover with foil and cook for 1½ hours. If casserole is going to be served immediately, add chestnuts after the first 45 minutes.

◗ ❊ May be made up to this point the day before or may be frozen.

To re-heat – allow casserole to defrost completely. Add frozen or tinned chestnuts and put in oven for 45 minutes - 1 hour, stirring occasionally until piping hot.

Sprinkle chopped parsley on top and serve.

Cook's tip: To make shallots easier to peel, first plunge them in boiling water for 5 minutes.

TOASTED SESAME DUCHESSE POTATOES

1 tin "Smash"
900ml (1½ pts) milk
50g (2oz) butter or "Olivio"
2 eggs – beaten
oil
8 tsp sesame seeds
salt and pepper
Oven: 190°C, 375°F, Gas Mark 5

My husband loves mashed potato and considers himself a real gourmet on the subject. If you mentioned "Smash" to him, he would have a fit. When creating this recipe, I tried many different variations of "the real thing" (which was very time consuming) and "Smash". I then tested them out on my husband and guess what? He couldn't tell the difference.

Make "Smash" according to instructions, using 8 scoops of "Smash" and substitute milk for water. Add butter or "Olivio", beaten eggs and season generously.

Brush 8 ramekin dishes with oil, put potato inside and sprinkle a teaspoon of sesame seeds on top of each one.

◗ ❊ May be made in advance and frozen at this stage.

Put in the oven for 25 minutes. May be served in ramekin dishes or turned out and served sesame side up.

Cook's tips: Even though the "Smash" tin is handy for storage don't be tempted to hang on to it. What could be worse than being found out to be a cheat? Around Christmas, some of the supermarkets stock frozen duchesse potatoes. You could use these instead and sprinkle sesame seeds on top.

HARICOTS VERTS WITH SAUTÉED ONIONS

2 tbsp oil

3 large onions – sliced

900g (2lbs) frozen "Fine Whole Green Beans"

salt and pepper

I usually find frozen green beans rather soggy, but cooked in this way they keep their crunch and taste delicious.

Heat the oil in a wok or large frying pan. Add onions and sauté until golden. Add beans and continue to cook tossing occasionally for approximately 8 minutes until beans are cooked through. Season and serve.

Cook's tip: Do not de-frost the beans, cook from frozen.

CHRISTMAS TIRAMISU

110g (4oz) raisins

slug brandy (approx 3 tbsp)

425ml (¾pt) red wine

1 mulled wine sachet (or 2 tsp cloves and 2 cinnamon sticks)

4 tbsp sugar

300ml (½pt) double cream

250g (9oz) Mascarpone

400ml (¾pt) carton ready-made custard – preferably fresh but long-life will do

200g packet Boudoirs Biscuits (Ladies Fingers)

1 tsp cinnamon

A wonderfully alcoholic pudding to send you into a blissful haze for the rest of the day.

Mix raisins in a bowl with brandy and leave to stand. Heat wine with sachet (or spices) and 2tbsp sugar in a saucepan for 10 minutes, stirring occasionally. Meanwhile, whisk cream with remaining 2 tbsp sugar until stiff. Add Mascarpone and custard and whisk for a few seconds until blended.
Discard sachet (or spices) from wine. Briefly dip Boudoirs biscuits into mulled wine (do not soak too much or else they will disintegrate).

Place half the Boudoirs biscuits in the bottom of a serving bowl, followed by half the raisins in brandy and half the cream mixture. Repeat the same process with the second half of the ingredients. Sift cinnamon on top and chill for at least 1 hour.

◖ ❄ May be made the day before or may be frozen.

Cook's tip: Any cheap red wine may be used for this recipe but try to remain sober while making it!

ORDER OF PREPARATION IF MAKING IN ADVANCE:

1. Make pheasant casserole up to ❄ and cool completely.
2. Make potatoes up to ❄ and cool.
3. Make tiramisu.
4. Make feta tarts up to ❄

The day before:
5. Take everything, except green beans, out of freezer. Once defrosted keep in fridge.

On the day:
6. Re-heat pheasant.
7. Put potatoes in oven when needed.
8. Put feta tarts in oven when needed.
9. Cook beans.

ORDER OF PREPARATION IN UNDER 2 HOURS:

1. Soak raisins and make mulled wine.
2. Prepare pheasant casserole and cook as necessary.
3. Make tiramisu.
4. Prepare potatoes and put in oven when needed.
5. Prepare tarts and put in oven when needed.
6. Cook beans.

A "CLASSY" BRUNCH

It has become a tradition over the past ten years, that all the family come to us for lunch on Boxing Day. Numbers range from 20 to 30, depending on how many distant cousins turn up. For eight of these years I would struggle with a huge roast, bribe someone to carve it and spend hours preparing and cooking hundreds of different vegetables. Two years ago, when I announced that we were having "brunch", I was nearly ex-communicated. I made all the recipes below, mainly in advance, so that I could have a long lie-in to recover from my Christmas Day hang-over. It was the most relaxing Boxing Day I have ever had. When the complimentary letters and phone calls came in afterwards, I realised that a divorce was no longer imminent and that brunch was going to become a regular Boxing Day event. The only problem now is that the numbers have gone up from 30 to 40!

SMOKED SALMON MOUSSE WITH PITTA TRIANGLES
LUXURY KEDGEREE
MARMALADE GLAZED VENISON SAUSAGES
SPINACH PEPPERONI AND MUSHROOM AU GRATIN
CROISSANT, APRICOT AND BUTTER PUDDING WITH A
BRANDIED APRICOT SAUCE

♀ New World Fizz. Recommendation – Seaview Pinot Chardonnay from Australia
♀ A New World Semillon and a fruity easy going red. Recommendations – Peter Lehmann Semillon from Australia and Balbi Malbec from Argentina

SMOKED SALMON MOUSSE WITH PITTA TRIANGLES

This is ideal to have with your Fizz and can be served as a dip with the pitta triangles.

Put all ingredients except the pitta in a food processor until smooth. Turn out into a serving bowl.

◗ ❋ May be made the day before or may be frozen.

Cut pitta into triangles, 6 per round, and place on a baking tray in the oven for 10 minutes. Serve on a platter with the smoked salmon mousse in the middle and allow people to help themselves.

Cook's tip: This can also be served with bread sticks, French bread or cheese crackers.

200g (7oz) smoked salmon trimmings
200ml crème fraîche – low fat if you're feeling healthy
100g (3½oz) Greek yoghurt
juice of ½ lemon
1 handful fresh dill
pepper
2 packets round pitta bread (16 in total)
Oven: 190ºC, 375ºF, Gas Mark 5

LUXURY KEDGEREE

This is great for a large party as it can be made in advance and frozen. I have added prawns and cream, which are optional, to make this kedgeree extra special.

1 large onion – chopped

110g (4oz) butter or "Olivio"

½ tsp curry powder

350g (12oz) long-grain rice

850ml (1½ pts) boiling water

800g (1lb 12oz) smoked haddock fillet – skinned and cut into chunks

200g (7oz) prawns – fresh or frozen and de-frosted – optional

2 lemons

4 hard boiled eggs

150ml (¼pt) single cream – optional

2 handfuls chopped parsley or coriander

75g (3oz) watercress

salt and pepper

Melt half the butter or "Olivio" in a very large saucepan, add the chopped onion and fry gently for 3 minutes to soften. Add curry powder and rice and continue cooking for another 2 minutes. Add boiling water, allow to simmer gently for 10 minutes then add smoked haddock and continue to cook for a further 10 minutes until rice is tender and liquid is absorbed. If making in advance, see instructions below. If serving immediately, add prawns, juice of half a lemon, remaining butter or Olivio, chopped hard boiled eggs, cream, half the herbs and season. Leave on heat to warm through for a couple of minutes and serve as below.

◑ ❋ May be prepared up to this point the day before or may be frozen.

To re-heat – de-frost if necessary, put in an oven-proof serving dish and toss together with the prawns, lemon juice and cover. Put in oven: 190ºC, 375ºF, Gas Mark 5 for 40 minutes or microwave on high for 15 minutes, stirring half way through, until piping hot. Chop hard boiled eggs and mix in with cream, half the chopped parsley or coriander and season.

To serve – cut remaining lemons into wedges, sprinkle remaining herbs on top of kedgeree and decorate with watercress.

Cook's tip: Watch the rice carefully while cooking for the last few minutes and cut with a metal spoon to separate and see how much water is left. It is important that all the water is absorbed but that it does not burn.

MARMALADE GLAZED VENISON SAUSAGES

Cooking sausages in marmalade gives them a wonderful orange flavoured glaze which people think you must have spent hours achieving when, in fact, you haven't.

16 venison sausages or any other exciting variety that you can get hold of, e.g. wild boar, pork and leek, spicy pork

4 heaped tbsp marmalade

Oven: 200ºC, 400ºF, Gas Mark 6

Prick sausages with a fork and put in a roasting tin in one layer and toss together with the marmalade. Cook in oven for 1 hour until sausages are cooked through, basting with the marmalade every now and then. Drain off fat just before the end of cooking. Serve with the marmalade glaze.

Cook's tip: If you only have room in the oven for a small tin and the sausages are not in one layer, allow more time for cooking.

SPINACH, PEPPERONI AND MUSHROOM AU GRATIN

1.5kg (3lbs) frozen leaf spinach – de-frosted and drained

150g (5oz) pepperoni – thinly sliced

200g (7oz) mushrooms – sliced

1 tub (300g–350g) ready-made carbonara or cheese sauce

110g (4oz) Cheddar or other cheese – grated

Oven: 190°C, 375°F, Gas Mark 5

This deliciously cheesy spinach dish is made slightly spicy by the pepperoni. If you prefer, you can use chopped ham or chopped fried bacon instead.

Mix all ingredients, except half the grated cheese, together. Put in a large gratin dish and sprinkle remaining cheese on top.

◗ May be prepared up to this point the day before.

Put in oven for 40 minutes.

Cook's tip: This is also ideal served as a starter for a dinner party, cooked in individual gratin dishes or ramekins. It would also be suitable for a casual lunch or supper (the above quantities would be enough for 4 as a main course), served with a salad and warm bread.

CROISSANT, APRICOT AND BUTTER PUDDING WITH A BRANDIED APRICOT SAUCE

8 croissants

75g (3oz) butter or Olivio

apricot jam or conserve

250g (9oz) ready to eat dried apricots

150ml (¼pt) double cream

300ml (½pt) milk

4 eggs

2 tbsp brown sugar

large slug brandy (approx. 5 tbsp or more)

400ml (¾pt) carton ready-made custard – preferably fresh but long-life will do

Oven: 180°C, 350°F, Gas Mark 4

You can't have brunch without croissants, so I have used them in this indulgent version of a bread and butter pudding.

Grease an oven-proof serving dish.

Cut croissants in half horizontally and spread each with butter or Olivio and apricot jam. Sandwich together and put in one layer in the dish (you may have to squeeze them together to get them in – it should be a tight fit). Using half the quantity of apricots, push in between croissants. Beat cream, milk and eggs together and pour over croissants. Sprinkle brown sugar on top.

To make sauce – roughly chop remaining apricots and put in a bowl together with brandy and custard.

◗ May be made up to this point the day before.

Put croissants in oven for 40 minutes. Gently heat sauce and serve.

ORDER OF PREPARATION IF MAKING IN ADVANCE:

The day before:
1. Make smoked salmon mousse.
2. Make kedgeree up to ✳
3. Make spinach up to ◗
4. Make croissant pudding up to ◗

In the morning:
5. Cook sausages as necessary.
6. Re-heat kedgeree.
7. Cook spinach.

8. Heat pitta triangles.
9. Cook croissant pudding.

ORDER OF PREPARATION IN UNDER 2 HOURS:
1. Make smoked salmon mousse and heat pitta triangles as needed.
2. Prepare sausages and put in oven as necessary.
3. Prepare spinach and cook as needed.
4. Make kedgeree.
5. Make croissant pudding.

FESTIVE FARE

This is an ideal menu to serve around Christmas time and makes a welcome change from the "on-going" turkey!

BLINIS WITH SMOKED SALMON AND DILL FROMAGE FRAIS
STUFFED PHEASANT BREASTS WRAPPED IN BACON
POTATO AND CELERIAC DAUPHINOISE
BRUSSELS SPROUTS WITH TOASTED ALMONDS
MULLED WINE FRUIT COMPOTE WITH CRÈME BRULÉE

A crisp white and a warm spicy red. Recommendation – Montana, Marlborough, Sauvignon Blanc from New Zealand and Penfolds, Bin 2, Shiraz Mourvèdre from Australia

BLINIS WITH SMOKED SALMON AND DILL FROMAGE FRAIS

A very impressive starter but time consuming if you make the blinis yourself – don't let on to your guests that you haven't.

Chop half the fresh dill and mix with fromage frais and dill sauce. Grill or toast blinis/"Pikelets" as instructions on packet. Put slices of smoked salmon on top, followed by a blob of dill fromage frais and finally scatter over remaining sprigs of dill. Serve on individual plates with the salad leaves arranged around one side of the plate and a slice of lemon.

Cook's tips: Pikelets are like thin crumpets and make a good substitute for blinis. Blinis can be frozen, so if you do come across them, buy them and store in the freezer until needed.

8 ready–made blinis or 1 packet (8) "Pikelets" (Blinis can be bought from large branches of Sainsburys and specialist delis)
bunch fresh dill
200g (7oz) fromage frais
½ jar (approx 90g) dill sauce or dill mustard
400g (14oz) smoked salmon
100g bag mixed salad leaves
1 lemon – cut into 8 slices

STUFFED PHEASANT BREASTS WRAPPED IN BACON

The pheasant season is from September to January, but you can always buy and freeze them during this period, and use them when needed. I have used boneless breasts in this recipe as they are the most tender part of the pheasant and easy to manage. Boneless breasts can be bought from large supermarkets and some butchers. The pheasant, bacon and stuffing combines a wonderful combination of textures and flavours. It looks very impressive when sliced and fanned out on individual plates, however, if you find this last minute preparation a fiddle, just leave the breasts whole.

Make stuffing as instructions on packet and leave to cool.
Peel onions and garlic and put in a food processor or liquidizer with thyme leaves and redcurrant jelly until smooth. Add wine and season to make the sauce.

Cut slits in the pheasant breasts lengthways. Divide the stuffing between the breasts and fold up. Wrap three rashers of bacon around each breast with the bacon over-lapping at the bottom. (The breasts should be virtually covered by the bacon and there is no need to secure the bacon with cocktail sticks.) Put in

Packet of parsley and thyme stuffing mix – approx 85g
2 medium onions
2 garlic cloves
1 handful fresh thyme
½ small jar redcurrant jelly
600ml (1 pt) red wine
8 pheasant breasts
24 rashers streaky rindless bacon
salt and pepper
Oven: 190ºC, 375ºF, Gas Mark 5

an oven proof dish and pour red wine mixture on top. Leave to marinate for at least 1 hour.

◑ May be made up to this point earlier in the day or the day before.

Cook in oven, uncovered, for 50 minutes starting with the bottom side up and turning half way through cooking.

To serve – slice each breast and fan out on the plates. Pour the wine sauce on top.

Cook's tip: Sharpen your knife before slicing the pheasant – it will make it far easier.

POTATO AND CELERIAC DAUPHINOISE

700g (1½ lbs) potatoes

700g (1½ lbs) celeriac

1 carton (284ml / ½pt) fresh chicken stock

275ml (½ pt) milk

75g (3oz) Cheddar – grated

salt and pepper

Oven: 180ºC, 350ºF, Gas Mark 4

The addition of celeriac to this potato dauphinoise makes it unusual and quite delicious. It is only the root of the celeriac which is eaten. The top, which is rarely sold with it, looks like an undeveloped head of celery. Contrary to popular belief, celeriac and celery are not part of the same plant.

Grease an oven-proof gratin or serving dish. Scrub potatoes and peel celeriac. Slice in a food processor and put layers of potato and celeriac into the dish. Mix stock with milk and pour over. Season and cover with foil. Cook in oven for 1¾ hours. After the first hour sprinkle with cheese and continue cooking uncovered.

◑ May be made up to this point the day before, cooled and refrigerated overnight.

To re-heat – put in oven uncovered for 30 minutes.

Cook's tip: If you are using a food processor, grate the cheese first, then you can slice the potatoes without having to wash it up in-between.

BRUSSELS SPROUTS WITH TOASTED ALMONDS

1½ kg (3 lbs) brussels sprouts (can be bought already trimmed from supermarkets)

40g (1½ oz) butter or "Olivio"

100g (4oz) flaked almonds (or you can buy already toasted flaked almonds from some supermarkets)

salt and pepper

I always think brussels sprouts can be a bit boring but they are transformed into something far more exciting with the addition of the toasted almonds. If you buy already trimmed sprouts and ready toasted almonds, this cuts the time down considerably.

To toast almonds (if necessary) – spread nuts on a baking tray and place under a hot grill for a few minutes until golden brown.

Trim the base of the sprouts and remove outer leaves. Put into boiling, salted water and cook for 10-15 minutes. Drain and toss in butter/"Olivio", toasted almonds and season.

Cook's tip: If you have any sprouts or potato and celeriac dauphinoise left over, make them into a soup. Just add stock, simmer for 10 minutes and blend in a food processor or liquidizer.

MULLED WINE FRUIT COMPOTE WITH CRÈME BRULÉE

400ml (¾ pt) red wine

1 mulled wine sachet (or 2 tsp cloves and 2 cinnamon sticks)

3 tbsp castor or granulated sugar

750g (1½ lbs) mixture dried fruits (ready to eat), e.g. apricots, pears, pitted prunes, figs

2 eggs

300ml (½ pt) double cream

400ml (¾ pt) carton ready-made custard – preferably fresh but long-life will do

4 tbsp brown sugar

Oven: 190ºC, 375ºF, Gas Mark 5

The smell of mulled wine always reminds me of Christmas. Mulled wine sachets are now available from most supermarkets and are very effective.

Heat wine with mulled wine sachet or spices and 3 tbsp sugar for 10 minutes. Remove sachet or cloves and cinnamon and add fruit. Allow to gently simmer for a further 10 minutes. Leave to marinate for 1 hour or overnight.
Put fruit into an oven-proof serving dish. Beat eggs and mix with cream and custard. Pour over fruit and sprinkle brown sugar on top.

❄ May be made up to this point earlier in the day.

Cook in oven for 30 minutes.

Cook's tip: Make up double quantity of the mulled wine so that you can have a drink while you're cooking!

ORDER OF PREPARATION IF MAKING IN ADVANCE:

The day before:
1. Make pheasant recipe up to ◐
2. Make potato and celeriac dauphinoise up to ◐

Earlier on the day:
3. Prepare compote up to ❄
4. Trim sprouts and toast almonds if necessary.

In the evening:
5. Prepare blini recipe.
6. Cook pheasant.
7. Re-heat potatoes.
8. Cook sprouts.
9. Cook pudding.

ORDER OF PREPARATION IN 2 UNDER HOURS:
1. Make and cook potato and celeriac dauphinoise.
2. Prepare pheasant and cook when necessary.
3. Prepare pudding and cook when necessary.
4. Prepare sprouts and cook as needed.
5. Prepare blini recipe.

TOTALLY VEGETARIAN

Whether or not you are a vegetarian, you will enjoy these delicious recipes. With so many people eating less meat, there is more and more demand for exciting vegetarian dishes. In this menu, the starter and main course can be adapted to include meat or fish for those who can't do without it.

♀ Southern Italian red. Recommendation – Castel del Monte Rosso

WARM SPICY LENTIL AND VEGETARIAN SAUSAGE SALAD
ON A BED OF LAMB'S LETTUCE
AUBERGINE AND MUSHROOM RAGOUT WITH A GNOCCHI,
BASIL AND MOZZARELLA TOPPING
CARROT AND CORIANDER TIMBALES
GRILLED ARTICHOKES AND PEPPERS
WARM, INDIVIDUAL APPLE AND DATE TARTS WITH COINTREAU CUSTARD

WARM SPICY LENTIL AND VEGETARIAN SAUSAGE SALAD ON A BED OF LAMB'S LETTUCE

Vegetarian sausages are widely available these days and I was very pleasantly surprised by how good they taste.

Cook sausages as instruction on packet and slice thickly.

☼ May be done earlier in the day.

Heat 2 tbsp of the oil in a large saucepan, add spring onions and chilli and gently fry for about 2 minutes until softened. Add lentils, sausages and cumin and gently heat through.

Mix chopped tomatoes with balsamic vinegar and remaining olive oil. Add to pan with lentil mixture and season. Serve on a bed of lamb's lettuce.

6 – 8 vegetarian sausages
6 tbsp olive oil
8 spring onions – sliced
2 red chillies – de-seeded and finely chopped or a few drops chilli sauce
2 tins (approx 400g) lentils – drained
4 tomatoes – chopped
150g (5oz) lamb's lettuce – or other lettuce may be used
2 tsp cumin seeds
2 tbsp balsamic vinegar

AUBERGINE AND MUSHROOM RAGOUT WITH A GNOCCHI, BASIL AND MOZZARELLA TOPPING

2 tbsp olive oil
2 large onions – sliced
3 cloves garlic – crushed
2 large or 3 medium aubergines – cut into chunks
2 handfuls fresh basil
2 jars (440g each) pasta sauce e.g. Ragu, Dolmio or similar
300g (11oz) mushrooms – sliced
800g (1lb 12oz) ready-made gnocchi (either potato or semolina based)
200g (7oz) mozzarella – grated (you can buy bags of already grated mozzarella)
salt and pepper

Gnocchi are small Italian dumplings made from mashed potatoes, potato flour, semolina or polenta. I have used gnocchi in this recipe as not many people are aware that you can buy it ready made.

Heat oil in a large frying pan or wok, add onions and fry until softened. Add garlic, aubergines, a third of the basil (shredded) and pasta sauce and simmer gently, stirring occasionally for 35 minutes. Add mushrooms and continue to cook for a further 10 minutes. Season.

Meanwhile, cook gnocchi as instructions on packet and drain.

Put aubergine ragout into a large oven-proof serving dish. Put gnocchi on top (you may have to separate them if they have stuck together). Finish with grated mozzarella and another third of the basil (shredded). Put under a hot grill to brown, decorate with remaining basil leaves and serve.

◗ May be made up to the point before grilling the day before and kept in the fridge overnight.

To re-heat – put in oven: 190°C, 375°F, Gas Mark 5 for 30 minutes then decorate with remaining basil leaves.

N.B. This recipe may have the addition of chicken or fish, e.g. cod, monkfish, halibut, etc. Substitute 1 large or 2 medium aubergines for the chicken or fish and if using chicken, cut into strips and add with the onion, if using fish, cut into chunks and add with the aubergine.

Cook's tip: If you've always sprinkled salt on aubergine and left it for 30 minutes – don't – it's a waste of time and effort as it doesn't taste any different.

CARROT AND CORIANDER TIMBALES

oil
grated Parmesan
2 garlic cloves
1 handful fresh coriander
1kg (2lbs 4oz) frozen carrots – de-frosted
200ml crème fraîche – the reduced fat type may be used
5 eggs
salt and pepper
Oven: 200°C, 400°F, Gas Mark 6

These timbales are very impressive but much more simple to make than your guests will imagine.

Brush 11-12 ramekin dishes with oil and sprinkle Parmesan around the bottom and sides. Put garlic and coriander (with stalks) in a food processor to chop. Add carrots, crème fraîche, eggs, salt and pepper and process until smooth. Pour into ramekin dishes, place on a baking tray and cook in oven for 45 minutes. Either serve immediately in ramekin dishes or leave to cool.

◗ ❄ May be made up to this point the day before or may be frozen.

Slide a knife around each timbale and turn out onto the palm of your hand and then place, with top facing down, on a baking tray. Sprinkle with a little Parmesan and put back in oven for a further 10-15 minutes. This makes enough for 11-12 people.

Cook's tip: If you are planning on freezing these, it's a good idea to turn them out of the ramekins first otherwise you won't be able to use the ramekins while they are in the freezer.

GRILLED ARTICHOKE AND PEPPERS

2 tins artichoke hearts

3 red peppers

200g bag mixed salad leaves

8 tbsp ready-made dressing

salt and pepper

I love artichokes but find fresh ones can be a hassle to eat. Tinned artichokes are far easier. All you have to do is open the tin, drain and eat them.

Drain the artichokes and cut in half. Brush cut sides with olive oil and put under a hot grill for approximately 4 minutes until golden. Cut peppers into quarters and remove stalk and seeds. Put, skin side up, under a very hot grill until the skin starts to bubble and go black. Plunge into cold water and peel off skin. Put artichokes and peppers into a bowl and toss in dressing.

◗ May be made up to this point the day before and left to marinate in fridge.

Serve in a large salad bowl or platter tossed into salad leaves.

Cook's tip: You must have the courage to leave the peppers under the grill long enough for the skins to turn really black as this will make them much easier to peel. Alternatively, you can grill them lightly and leave the skins on.

INDIVIDUAL WARM APPLE AND DATE TARTS WITH BRANDY CUSTARD

1 packet (375g) ready-rolled puff pastry

4 large eating apples

4 tsp brown sugar

100g (3½oz) chopped dates

3 tbsp golden syrup

BRANDY CUSTARD

1 carton (400ml / ¾pt) ready-made custard – preferably fresh but long-life will do

large slug brandy (5 tbsp or more) – other liqueurs may be used instead, e.g. Cointreau, Grand Marnier, Drambuie.

Oven: 220ºC, 425ºF, Gas Mark 7

It's amazing how somthing so delectable can be so easy.

Roll out pastry thinly to form a square. Using a cup or bowl approx 11cm (4½") in diameter as a guide, cut out 8 circles. Put on a greased baking tray and turn up the edges slightly to form a rim. Make sure the baking tray is greased well as the golden syrup has a habit of dripping down the sides and sticking to the bottom. There is no need to peel the apples. Use an apple corer to remove the centre of the apples and cut into thin slices (alternatively, cut into quarters, core and slice). Arrange slices from half an apple on each tart and sprinkle with brown sugar. Bake in oven for 25 minutes. Mix chopped dates with golden syrup. Spoon mixture on top of tarts and, if serving immediately, put back in oven to warm. If making in advance, see instructions below.

To make brandy custard – mix custard with brandy and heat gently.

◗ The tarts may be made the day before.

To re-heat – put in oven: 180ºC, 350ºF, Gas Mark 4 for 10-15 minutes.

ORDER OF PREPARATION IF MAKING IN ADVANCE:

The day before:
1. Make ragout up to ◗
2. Make carrot and coriander timbales up to ✳
3. Prepare artichokes and peppers up to ◗
4. Make apple tarts.

Earlier on the day:
5. Cook the sausages.

In the evening:
6. Make starter.
7. Re-heat ragout and ᵇbales when necessary.
8. Toss artichokes and peppers into leaves.
9. Re-heat tarts as needed.

ORDER OF PREPARATION IN UNDER 2 HOURS:
1. Make tarts and re-heat when needed.
2. Make timbales, turn out when cool enough to handle and re-heat.
3. Make ragout.
4. Prepare artichokes and peppers and toss in leaves before serving.
5. Make starter.

WINTER WARMER

The following recipes are highly alcoholic and ideal for a winter dinner party. They include rather a lot of cheating enabling you to prepare the whole menu in under an hour.

WILD MUSHROOM SOUP WITH OLIVE CROSTINI
OVEN ROAST RUMP STEAK WITH PORT, MUSTARD AND CARAMELISED ONIONS
HORSERADISH MASH
BEETROOT DAUPHINOISE
STICKY TOFFEE PUDDING WITH A RUM, RAISIN AND TOFFEE SAUCE

♀ A full bodied Southern French red. Recommendation – Mas Cal Demoura, Coteaux du Languedoc – 1993 – From France

WILD MUSHROOM SOUP WITH OLIVE CROSTINI

The chunks of mushrooms in this soup will convince your guests that you made it from scratch but don't feel guilty for stealing all the credit. Even people who don't like olives, usually like the olive crostini – they seem to take on a different flavour served in this way.

First make crostini – cut baguette into 24 thin slices and put under a hot grill until golden on both sides.

Empty cartons of soup into a large saucepan and destroy the evidence! Wash mushrooms thoroughly. Either slice, cut in half or leave the mushrooms whole if they are small. Add to soup with crushed garlic, sherry and seasoning.

☼ May be prepared up to this point earlier in the day.

◗ The crostini may be made a few days in advance and kept in an air-tight container.

Spread one side of the crostini with olive paste. Heat the soup gradually until piping hot. Pour into bowls and float 3 olive crostini in each bowl.

Cook's tip: Mushrooms can sometimes just be wiped clean as they tend to absorb water if they are washed. Wild mushrooms, however, are often full of grit and grass so will need washing thoroughly and drained well on kitchen roll.

---

3 cartons "New Covent Garden" mushroom soup

250g (9oz) wild mushrooms – choose a mixture, e.g. chanterelles, shiitake, oyster

1 garlic clove – crushed

large slug of dry sherry – approx. 4 tbsp

salt and pepper

OLIVE CROSTINI

1 baguette (a thin French stick)

½ jar (approx. 80g) black olive paste

OVEN ROAST RUMP STEAK WITH PORT, MUSTARD AND CARAMELISED ONIONS

6 tbsp olive oil

4 large onions – sliced

4 level tbsp brown sugar

8 rump steaks – 175g-200g (6oz-7oz) each – fat removed

8 tbsp port (or 4 tbsp port and 4 tbsp water may be used)

2 tbsp grain mustard

salt and pepper

Oven: 230ºC, 450ºF, Gas Mark 8

Steak can be difficult to cook for a dinner party when you have to stand watching it by the grill. This method of cooking means you can stick it in the oven and forget about it – but not for too long.

Heat 2 tbsp of the olive oil in a frying pan and quickly brown steaks to seal –approximately 20 seconds on each side. Leave to cool.

❋ May be done earlier in the day.

Put sliced onion in a large roasting dish and mix with the remaining olive oil and brown sugar. Put in oven for 45 minutes, tossing half way though cooking. Mix port with mustard, salt and pepper. Place steaks on top of caramelised onions and pour port and mustard on top. Put back in oven for a further 10-15 minutes.

To serve – cut each piece of steak into thin strips and fan out on individual plates with onions in the middle and juices from the dish poured over.

Cook's tip: You will need a very sharp knife to slice the steak. Serving it this way looks very effective but if you find it too much to do at the last minute, just leave it whole with the onions piled on top.

HORSERADISH MASH

1.5kg (3lbs 5oz) potatoes

1 jar (approx 185g) creamed horseradish

3 tbsp olive oil

275ml (½pt) milk

2 garlic cloves – crushed

salt and pepper

Flavoured mashes are very trendy. The horseradish in this one goes very well with the steak.

Peel potatoes and boil until soft. Drain and mash together with remaining ingredients.

❋ May be made earlier in the day.

To re-heat – microwave on high for 8 minutes, stirring half way through. More milk may need to be added during re-heating to maintain a creamy consistency.

Cook's tip: Make sure the potatoes really are very soft before draining otherwise you'll have great difficulties trying to mash them.

BEETROOT DAUPHINOISE

1kg (2lbs 4oz) natural cooked beetroot

200ml crème fraîche – the low fat variety may be used

2 tsp French mustard

3 tbsp grated Parmesan

salt and pepper

Oven: 190ºC, 375ºF, Gas Mark 5

In this country beetroot is usually served cold in salads. This hot beetroot recipe makes an interesting vegetable dish with the most beautiful colours.

Drain and slice beetroot. Mix in a large bowl with the crème fraîche, mustard, salt and pepper. Put into an oven-proof serving dish. Sprinkle over Parmesan and cover with foil.

❋ May be prepared up to this point earlier in the day.

Cook in oven for 30 minutes.

Cook's tips: Buying ready cooked beetroot saves a huge amount of time but make sure you buy natural beetroot rather than the type in vinegar.

STICKY TOFFEE PUDDING WITH A RUM, RAISIN AND TOFFEE SAUCE

2 toffee or ginger cakes (McVitie's or other brands)

1 bottle (approx. 400g) toffee sauce – "Smuckers" recommended

150ml (¼pt) single cream

4 heaped tbsp raisins

large slug rum (approx 6 tbsp or more!)

Oven: 190°C, 375°F, Gas Mark 5

This recipe is certainly not in the "Weight Watchers Cook Book" but it is a wonderfully alcoholic pudding, which only takes a few minutes to make.

Cut both cakes in half horizontally. With a round pastry cutter (approx 7cm/3" in diameter) cut out 8 rounds. The remaining bits of cake can be discarded or you can have a nibble as you cook. Put the 8 rounds in an oven-proof serving dish.

Mix toffee sauce (you will probably have to heat the bottle to get it out as it is usually very thick) with the cream, raisins and rum. Pour over toffee puddings and cover with foil.

◖ May be made up to this point the day before.

Put sticky toffee puddings in oven for 15 minutes and serve.

Cook's Tip: Don't feel guilty about the cheating – just relax and enjoy it.

ORDER OF PREPARATION IF MAKING IN ADVANCE:

The day before:
1. Make sticky toffee puddings up to ◖
2. Make crostini.

Earlier on the day:
3. Prepare soup up to ☼
4. Prepare steak up to ☼
5. Prepare horseradish mash up to ☼
6. Prepare beetroot dauphinoise up to ☼

In t' evening:
7. Finish off steak recipe and put in oven as needed.
8. Finish off soup.
9. Cook beetroot and re-heat mash as needed.
10. Put sticky toffee pudding in oven while eating main course.

ORDER OF PREPARATION IN 1 HOUR:
1. Prepare soup and heat when necessary.
2. Prepare steak recipe and cook when needed.
3. Make beetroot dauphinoise.
4. Make sticky toffee pudding and put in oven during main course.
5. Make horseradish mash.

AN ALTERNATIVE CHRISTMAS

If the thought of all the family coming over on Christmas Day sends you into a cold sweat and terminal depression – here's your remedy. This menu is ideal for the maverick host who wants to ring in the changes but keep some of the traditional seasonal fare. All the recipes are incredibly quick and easy and will save you having to get up at five in the morning to start cooking. Apart from the starter, they can be prepared in advance and frozen, enabling you to have a lie-in and actually enjoy the in-laws, nieces, nephews. aunts and uncles later.

A fruity New World white and a Pinot Noir. Recommendation – Lindemans Cawarra Colombard Chardonnay from Australia and Franciscan Pinnacles Pinot Noir from California

MANGO, MELON, PRAWN AND MINT SALAD
TURKEY ROULADE WITH STILTON AND SPINACH
RED CABBAGE WITH APPLE AND SPICES
POTATO AND LEEKS À LA BOULANGÈRE
CHRISTMAS PUDDING ICE CREAM
FILO MINCE TARTS

MANGO, MELON, PRAWN AND MINT SALAD

200g (7oz) prawns – fresh or frozen
2 ripe mangoes
1 medium melon
2 tbsp olive oil
1 tbsp balsamic vinegar
2 handfuls fresh mint
salt and pepper

This is a lovely refreshing salad combining wonderful flavours which won't fill you up before the main course.

De-frost prawns if frozen. Peel mangos and cut the flesh from either side of the stone, then cut each wedge of mango into 8 thin slices (there should be 24 slices in total). Reserve the remainder of the mango around the stone for the dressing. Cut melon in half and remove pips. Scoop out the melon flesh with a melon baller or cut into chunks.

To make dressing – cut the remaining mango from around the stone and put in a food processor or liquidizer with the oil, vinegar, salt, pepper and ¾ of the mint.

✳ May be prepared up to this point earlier in the day.

Arrange mango slices, melon balls and prawns on each plate. Pour over dressing and decorate with remaining mint leaves. Serve with warm bread – see Handy Hints page 6.

Cook's tip: If you are preparing the fruit earlier in the day, cover with cling-film and keep in the fridge.

TURKEY ROULADE WITH STILTON AND SPINACH

16 small turkey steaks or 8 turkey breast fillets
500g (1lb 2oz) chopped frozen spinach – de-frosted and drained
175g (6oz) Stilton
275ml (½pt) dry white wine
1 tub (300g-350g) ready-made cheese sauce
salt and pepper
Oven: 190ºC, 375ºF, Gas Mark 5

No more nightmares about cooking turkey – all you have to do on the day is put it in the oven for 40 minutes – heaven.

Lay the turkey steaks/breasts flat on a chopping board or work surface, cover with cling-film and flatten with a rolling pin. Place equal amounts of spinach and stilton on the turkey fillets and roll up tightly. Place in an oven-proof dish in one layer with the fold at the bottom.

● ❄ May be made up to this point in advance or may be frozen.

Pour wine and cheese sauce over turkey and season. Cover with foil and cook for 40 minutes.

To serve – slice roulades and arrange fanned out on each plate. Pour sauce on top.

Cook's tip: There is no need to secure with cocktail sticks or tie up with dental floss (as a friend once did but forgot to remove it). As long as the fold is at the bottom and they are packed quite closely together, they will keep their shape.

POTATO AND LEEK À LA BOULANGÈRE

1.5kg (3lbs 5oz) potatoes – scrubbed
2 leeks – thinly sliced
1 small tin (227g) chopped tomatoes
1 handful fresh chopped parsley
1 carton (284ml / ½pt) fresh concentrated chicken stock
salt and paprika
Oven: 180ºC, 350ºF, Gas Mark 4

Layers of potato and leek cooked in a chicken stock. They can be prepared in advance and need no last minute attention.

Grease an oven-proof dish. Slice potatoes (may be done in a food processor) and put in dish, layered with leeks, tomatoes, parsley, salt and paprika. Finish off with a layer of potatoes on top. Pour over stock, sprinkle with more paprika and parsley and cover with foil. Cook for 1¾ hours, removing the foil for the last half hour to allow the top to brown.

● ❄ May be made up to this point in advance or may be frozen and re-heated.

Cook's tip: If frozen, allow plenty of time to de-frost. Re-heat in oven for 30 minutes.

RED CABBAGE WITH APPLE AND SPICES

1 large red cabbage
2 large onions – thinly sliced
4 eating apples – cored and chopped but skin left on
3 tbsp brown sugar
3 tbsp vinegar
½ tsp cinnamon
½ tsp ground ginger
salt and pepper

Red cabbage is one of the few vegetables which I think tastes just as good, if not better, made in advance and re-heated.

Cut red cabbage into quarters, cut away the core and dice. Put into a large saucepan with all remaining ingredients. Cover the pan and cook gently for 1½ hours, stirring occasionally.

● ❄ May be made in advance or frozen.

To re-heat – either put in microwave on high for 7 minutes, stirring half way through, or put in oven: 190ºC, 375ºF, Gas Mark 5 for 30 minutes.

Cook's tip: I often make double quantities of this recipe and put half in the freezer for a later date.

CHRISTMAS PUDDING ICE CREAM

1 litre good quality vanilla
ice cream

1 jar (400g) mincemeat

slug brandy – approx. 4 tbsp

1 sprig holly

This makes a change from the traditional Christmas Pudding. So simple but always a favourite.

Allow ice cream to soften slightly. Put mincemeat in a large bowl and mix with brandy and ice cream. Turn into a pudding basin and freeze for at least 2 hours.

❋ May be frozen.

To serve – put bowl into a basin of hot water for a few seconds and run a palate knife round the inside of the bowl to loosen the sides. Turn ice cream onto a serving plate and decorate with holly.

Cook's tip: Once the ice cream has frozen, you can turn it out onto a serving plate and return to the freezer until you are ready to serve it.

FILO MINCE TARTS

1 packet fresh filo pastry or 8
sheets (measuring approx.
30cm x 18cm)

2 tbsp olive oil

1 orange

1 jar (400g) mincemeat

50g (2oz) flaked almonds

1 tbsp icing sugar

200g (7oz) Greek yoghurt or
crème fraîche

Oven: 190ºC, 375ºF, Gas Mark 5

Using filo pastry for these tarts makes them lighter and just a bit different.

Lay one sheet of filo out and lightly brush half of it with oil and fold in ½ to form a square. Brush ½ of this square with oil and fold in ½ again. Cut filo in ½ to form 2 squares and snip off the corners with scissors. Put in tart tins. Repeat this process until you have 16 tarts.

Zest orange rind and squeeze the juice out. Mix together in a bowl with mincemeat and flaked almonds. Put the mincemeat mixture into the tarts and cook in oven for 15 minutes.

◖ ❋ May be made up to this point in advance or may be frozen.

To re-heat – put back in oven for 10 minutes. Sieve icing sugar over the tarts. Serve warm with Greek yoghurt or crème fraîche.

Cook's tip: See Handy Hints page 6 for tips on filo pastry.

ORDER OF PREPARATION IF
MAKING IN ADVANCE:

The day before:
1. Make everything except starter up to ❋

Earlier in the day:
2. Prepare starter.

In the evening or at lunch time:
3. Cook turkey.
4. Re-heat potatoes and red cabbage.
5. Turn ice cream out of bowl and return to freezer until needed.
6. Arrange starter on plates.
7. Re-heat tarts when needed.

ORDER OF PREPARATION IN
UNDER 2 HOURS:
1. Make ice cream and hope that it freezes in time!
2. Prepare and cook potatoes.
3. Make red cabbage recipe.
4. Prepare turkey and cook when needed.
5. Make mince tarts.
6. Make starter.

INDEX